Essential Series

Springer

London
Berlin
Heidelberg
New York
Hong Kong
Milan
Paris
Tokyo

Also in this series:

John Vince
Essential Virtual Reality *fast*
1-85233-012-0

John Cowell
Essential Visual J++ 6.0 *fast*
1-85233-013-9

John Cowell
Essential Java 2 *fast*
1-85233-071-6

John Cowell
Essential Visual Basic 6.0 *fast*
1-85233-071-6

John Vince
Essential Computer Animation *fast*
1-85233-141-0

Aladdin Ayesh
Essential Dynamic HTML *fast*
1-85233-626-9

David Thew
Essential Access 2000 *fast*
1-85233-295-6

Ian Palmer
Essential Java 3D *fast*
1-85233-394-4

Matthew Norman
Essential ColdFusion *fast*
1-85233-315-4

Ian Chivers
Essential Linux *fast*
1-85233-408-8

Fiaz Hussain
Essential Flash 5.0 *fast*
1-85233-451-7

John Vince
Essential Mathematics for
Computer Graphics *fast*
1-85233-380-4

John Cowell
Essential VB .NET *fast*
1-85233-591-2

Simon Stobart
Essential PHP *fast*
1-85233-578-5

Fiaz Hussain
Essential Dreamweaver 4.0 *fast*
1-85233-573-4

Aladdin Ayesh
Essential UML *fast*
1-85233-413-4

Simon Stobart
Essential ASP .NET *fast*
1-85233-683-8

Ian Stephenson
Essential RenderMan *fast*
1-85233-608-0

John Cowell

Essential XHTML™
fast

**Creating Dynamic Web Sites
with XHTML and JavaScript**

 Springer

Author and Series Editor
John Cowell, BSc (Hons), MPhil, PhD
Department of Computer Science, De Montfort University, The Gateway,
Leicester LE1 9BH

British Library Cataloguing in Publication Data
Cowell, John, 1957–
  Essential XHTML fast : creating dynamic Web sites with
  XHTML and JavaScript. – (Essential series)
  1. XHTML (Document markup language)   2. JavaScript (Computer
  program langauge)   3. Web sites – Design
  I. Title   II. XHTML fast
  005.7'2
  ISBN 1852336846

Library of Congress Cataloging-in-Publication Data
A catalog record for this book is available from the Library of Congress

Essential series ISSN 1439-975X

ISBN 1-85233-684-6 Springer-Verlag London Berlin Heidelberg
a member of BertelsmannSpringer Science+Business Media GmbH
http://www.springer.co.uk

Typesetting: electronic text files prepared by the author
Printed and bound at The Cromwell Press, Trowbridge, Wiltshire
34/3830-543210 Printed on acid-free paper SPIN 10888379

Contents

Contents

Chapter

1

Why do I need XHTML?

Introduction

XHTML in common with HTML is a markup language which allows you to specify the format and appearance of Web pages. The browser interprets the XHTML text file and displays the page.

In January 2000, the World Wide Web Consortium (W3C) released the first version of the Extensible Hypertext Markup Language (XHTML) and announced that it would no longer support HTML as a standard.

The development of XHTML is inextricably linked with JavaScript, since although you can create form based applications in XHTML, the addition of JavaScript gives you much greater flexibility and allows you to create far more interactive documents.

This book covers all the aspects of XHTML and JavaScript that you need to create powerful interactive Web documents.

Why switch to XHTML?

If you are using HTML, you may feel that this does everything you want and that there is no point in changing. However, there are a lot of advantages to using XHTML:

- One of the main problems with HTML is that different browsers support different and incompatible versions of HTML, so our pages will appear to be different depending on the browser that is used. XHTML provides a standard which uses XML terminology.
- The Web designer can add his own elements to XHTML to provide specialized facilities. Any XHTML compatible browser will be able to understand the new elements and render the page correctly.

- XHTML is the standard for supporting content delivery to web-enabled phones, Personal Digital Assistants and other wireless devices, which render the XHTML to provide the display and interaction required.
- HTML documents contain the format of the document as well as its structure, that is features such as the fonts and colours used. XHTML uses style sheets which separate these formatting elements from the description of document structure. This makes it easier to ensure a common rendering on different browsers and different platforms.
- Recent advances in JavaScript are supported by XHTML and if you want to use the latest features, you need to upgrade to XHTML.

One reason which is often given for not upgrading to XHTML is that the user needs an up-to-date browser to be able to see documents which use the new features. Developers are still encouraged to develop alternative sites which can be viewed by very basic browsers, particularly for commercial sites where it is important not to turn customers away. However, now that the latest browsers are available free or at very low cost, most users tend to upgrade. Unlike the latest versions of applications such as word processors, browsers are still relatively small applications and the latest versions will run fast even on a modest computer.

What do I need?

Since XHTML files are just text, you only need a few basic tools to develop applications:

- A simple text editor for typing the XHTML documents. There are a number of tools available, such as HyperText Builder from PAKSoft but these inevitably tend to lag behind the latest developments in XHTML and they may not give you exactly what you want. A search for XHTML tools will produce a list of tools, some of which can be downloaded and used free. In this book I am assuming that you are using a simple text editor such as Notepad or WordPad. If you do use a word processor make sure that you save the XHTML file as simple text.

- You will need the latest versions of at least one browser, the most common are by Microsoft and Netscape, but browsers such as Opera have a dedicated following. A trial version of Opera is available free from www.opera.com. It is worthwhile checking that your XHTML is displayed in the same way using the most popular browsers, since although in theory there should not be a problem, XHTML is liable to change and the browsers may lag behind this.

- The XHTML validator tool is essential to check that your XHTML conforms to the standard. A validator is available on the W3C web site. We will look at this later.

Unlike many applications, you do not need the latest, fastest computer to write XHTML and JavaScript, the system requirements are very modest and you should not have a problem with any Pentium-based PC or similar vintage Unix or Linux based computer.

Is this book for you?

If you are an HTML programmer, you will find that many aspects of XHTML are the same, but that there are important differences which you need to take into account. In addition, XHTML offers many advantages over HTML which can help you to write more stable applications with a wide range of capabilities. Many HTML programmers are still applying formatting in-line in the document, so that every time an element occurs it needs to be formatted. This is not too much of an overhead for small Web sites, but as the number of documents increases, maintenance becomes a serious problem. A decision to change the size, font or colour of a header can be a major headache which takes hours to change. The use of Cascading Style Sheets (CSS) for formatting documents would allow this sort of change in seconds - and would ensure that you did not accidentally miss formatting a few headers. This book covers CSS, tables, frames, and forms and also how to use JavaScript to produce stunning interactive applications.

If you are not already an HTML developer, there is no point in learning HTML, which is quickly being replaced by XHTML. If you do learn HTML first there are a lot of aspects which you will have to unlearn when you make the switch. This book is not designed to give a detailed history lesson on the development of HTML, it aims to bring you up to speed so that within the first hour you will be writing XHTML applications and quickly moving onto more advanced topics such as CSS, frames, tables, forms and JavaScript.

This book covers all of the key aspects of XHTML and JavaScript and gives you everything you need to develop powerful Web applications *fast*.

How to use this book

The chapters in this book have been designed to follow each other in a logical sequence, but the examples are as self-contained as possible, so if you already have a background in XHTML or HTML and want to know how to use frames, you can move directly to that chapter without having to read all the preceding chapters.

The first seven chapters cover all the basic aspects that you need to develop interesting Web documents, and you will find all that you need there.

Chapters Eight to Ten deal with Cascading Style Sheets, frames and forms.

Chapters Eleven to Fourteen describe how to write and integrate JavaScript into your XHTML documents.

Pictures showing the running applications and listings of the XHTML and JavaScript are shown, so that you can follow the examples in detail, however the best way to learn any new language is to try the examples for yourself as you read the book. Programming, especially Web programming, can be a lot of fun, so don't limit yourself just to the examples, try different variations for yourself. In a book of this length or even in one four times the size every aspect cannot be covered, so experiment and have fun.

Don't type!

All of the program examples shown are available from the Essential Series Web site, www.essential-series.com – so you don't have to type any program examples. While you are at the site take a look at the other books which are available in the series.

Chapter 2

XML and XHTML

Introduction

The most common use of HTML is to create pages on the World Wide Web, although it can be used for developing local applications. It is a language which is used to describe the layout of documents and also allows you to do a variety of other jobs such as link to other documents, describe forms and produce emails. Since we can already do this with HTML why do we need XHTML? XML is another hot topic, but what is the relationship between XML and XHTML? Other markup languages such as SGML are also often talked about at the same time as XHTML, what are they? How does a scripting language such as JavaScript relate to XHTML?

The aim of this book is to help you to write XHTML and JavaScript as fast and easily as possible, but it is helpful to have an understanding of the relationship between these technologies and we are going to look at that in this chapter before beginning our first XHTML document.

HTML versions

The Hypertext Markup Language, HTML, was developed in the late 1980s by Tim Berners-Lee, a particle physicist who worked for the Conseil Européen pour la Recherche Nucléaire (CERN) in Switzerland, to allow scientists to exchange documents in a standard format. The formal definition of HTML is written in a meta-language, that is a language which is used to describe other languages, called the Standarized General Markup Language (SGML). SGML is defined in an international standard produced by the International Standards Organization, (ISO).

In 1993, when the World Wide Web, (WWW), was gaining popularity, CERN handed over the future development to an industrial consortium called the World Wide Web Consortium (W3C).

Version 1.0 was released in 1993, Version 4.0 was released in December 1997. The current version 4.01 was released in December 1999 and was not intended to be a radically different version to 4.0, instead it resolved a number of issues such as tightening the specification of numerous attributes.

In January 2000 when version 1.0 of XHTML was released the W3C announced that it was no longer supporting HTML as a standard, but was going to focus on XHTML and XML.

What is XML?

The Standard Generalized Markup Language (SGML) is a meta-language which can be used to describe markup languages. The markup language HTML is based on SGML. The main problem with SGML is that it is complex and difficult to use. The eXtensible Markup Language, XML, which is used to define XHTML, has most of the power and flexibility of SGML, but is far less complicated.

A document which describes ten key features of XML can be found on the W3C web site at www.w3.org/XML/1999/XML-in-10-points. The key features of this document, in particular those which relate to XHTML, are:

- XML is for structuring data. Structured data includes spreadsheets, address books, technical transactions and technical drawings. XML provides a set of rules for formatting structured data into a readable text format. XML ensures that the data is structured in an unambiguous way which is easy to generate and read. It is extensible, platform independent, and supports both internationalization and localization.
- XML looks a bit like HTML. XML uses tags and elements and attributes like HTML. HTML defines what these elements and attributes do, XML uses the tags to delimit pieces of data. The interpretation of that data is entirely up to the application, for example,

the <p> tag in an XML document may not indicate a paragraph, it can mean anything depending on the context.

- XML is text, but it is not meant to be read. Most applications such as spreadsheets store data in a binary format. XML files are always human readable text, which usually does not need to be read, but can be if a problem arises.
- XML is verbose by design. XML uses a text format which tends to use more disk space than binary formats for data, however, both disk space and memory are cheap and if required XML files can be compressed using a zip program. In addition, communications programs such as HTTP/1/1 can compress data before transmission and decompress it after transmission.
- XML is a family of technologies. It defines the common framework of all XML based documents. It includes a growing set of modules which offer additional services such as Xlink and XPointer. XLink specifies a common way of adding hyperlinks to any XML document. XPointer is a way of pointing to data inside an XML document. CSS, which describes style sheets for formatting documents, is applicable to all XML based documents not just XHTML. In addition, the DOM provides a standard set of methods if you wish to work with any XML based document using a programming language.
- XHTML has many of the same features as HTML, but its syntax has been changed to comply with the rules of XML. XHTML uses the syntax rules of XML, but adds meaning to that syntax, for example, the XML syntax defines that <p> is an element, XHTML gives a meaning to this and says that it stands for 'paragraph'.
- XML is license-free, platform-independent and well-supported. By using XML you will have access to a large and growing pool of widely supported tools.

What is XHTML?

XHTML is the successor to HTML and follows the syntax and requirements rules of XML. While it appears to be similar in syntax to HTML there are some important differences.

Before we look at creating an XHTML document it is important to look at some terminology, in particular the terms tag, element and attribute and also the syntax rules for XML, which also apply to XHTML, since it is an application of XML.

Tags, elements and attributes

XHTML is an application of XML and therefore XHTML uses XML terminology, in particular the terms:

- element;
- tag;
- attribute.

There are two types of elements: non-empty and empty elements. A non-empty element consists of an opening and closing tag and data which is placed within the tags, for example in Figure 2.1:

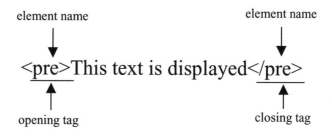

Figure 2.1 *Elements, tags and attributes.*

The name of the element is *pre*.

The opening tag consists of the element name enclosed within the angled brackets: <pre>.

The closing tag is the same as the opening tag except than the element name is preceded by the / character: </pre>

The data is the text enclosed within the opening and closing tags.

Empty elements do not have a closing tag, for example:

```
<br />
```

This element moves to a new line.

You can add attributes to the opening tag of many elements. Attributes are qualifiers which specify some non default behaviour. They always consist of a name-value pair, for example:

```
<a href = "http://www.essential-series.com/">Essential series home page</a>
```

This shows the opening and closing tags of the *a* element. The opening tag has one attribute. The name of the attribute is *href*, the value assigned to it is: http://www.essential-series.com/. There may be more than one attribute.

Empty elements may also have attributes, for example:

```
<img hetty = "hetty.gif" />
```

XML rules

The rules for writing XML and therefore XHTML elements are stricter than for HTML documents.

- XHTML is case sensitive. All tags must be written in lower case letters, for example:

```
<head>
```

- Every non-empty XHTML element must have a closing tag, for example:

```
<title>This appears on the browser title</title>
```

The closing tag is the same as the opening tag apart from the / in front of it. In earlier versions of HTML it was not mandatory to have a closing tag for all elements.

- Empty elements are those which do not have a closing tag, such as the *img* element. These are closed instead using a slightly different format, a single slash / is added before the closing >, for example:

```
<img hetty = "hetty.gif" />
```

- Attributes must be placed within quotation marks, for example:

```
<td align = "center" />
```

- Even attributes which do not have an obvious value must be assigned one, for example:

```
<d1 compact = "compact">
```

In HTML the assignment could have been omitted.

What is JavaScript?

A technology which is often misunderstood is JavaScript. It has some syntactic similarities to the Java programming language, but their capabilities are quite different. The earliest versions of JavaScript were called LiveScript and cynics claim that the name change was an attempt to benefit from the popularity of Java. Java applications which can be run within a browser environment are called applets. Java is a general, object-oriented programming language which supports multi-threaded code, networking and graphics. JavaScript is a scripting language, it does not support the items listed for Java, but can interact with the browser and the XHTML.

If you need to carry out mathematical operations, validate text, respond to events on forms or validate user input, you can use JavaScript. The *script* element is used, that is, the JavaScript is placed within an opening *<script>* tag and a closing *</script>* tag. In this way JavaScript is able to carry out activities which cannot be done in XHTML, and so the two complement each other.

There are a few alternative scripting languages to JavaScript. JScript is Microsoft's version of JavaScript and is virtually identical. VBScript is still fairly widely used, but it is diminishing in popularity, and Microsoft even state on their Web site that JScript is the preferred option.

Getting started

We have looked at some of the key terminology that is used with XHTML. The next stage is to start creating our first XHTML document. All you need is a simple editor and the latest copy of any browser.

A good way to work is to have the XHTML document you are working on open within the editor. Before you can view it in the browser, save it to a file with an html extension. When you have done this, run the browser and open the document. If there are errors, that is the document is not displayed or is not correctly displayed, click on the editor and make changes to the document. Remember to save it. To display the revised document in the browser, click the reload button. You may need to repeat this process a number of times to complete the document.

All the examples are available on the web site for you to download (www.essential-series.com). You will learn faster if you try them for yourself.

Chapter 3

Creating XHTML Documents

Introduction

XHTML is less forgiving that HTML in the structure and content of XHTML documents. In this chapter we are going to look at how to structure an XHTML document and use some basic elements and attributes. To check that the document is valid we are going to use the W3C validity check program. This useful application can verify that your XHTML has been written in accordance with the standard definitions.

Starting an XHTML document

There are three components which must be given to start an XHTML document:

- An XML statement.
- A DOCTYPE statement.
- A namespace statement.

We are going to look at these three in turn.

The XML statement

The XML statement announces that this document meets the specified XML standard and uses the specified character encoding. It is optional, but if it is used it may cause problems with some older browsers - Internet Explorer 5 and Netscape 4.7 or earlier, which are not XML aware.

If included, it must appear first in your document, on the first line, without any preceding white space. Note that there is no corresponding closing statement. It indicates that this document meets the XML specification, states the encoding scheme and whether there are declarations within another document which affect this document.

It has three attributes:

- version. Indicates the version of XML which the document complies with.
- encoding. The format used to encode the document.
- standalone. Whether the document depends on any other XML files to be valid.

For example, to show conformance with version 1.0 of the specification, the default UTF-8 encoding and no external declarations:

```
<?xml version = "1.0" encoding = "UTF-8" standalone = "no"?>
```

The version number is straightforward. If you are developing a new application, use the latest version available.

The *encoding* attribute is more complicated. The default is UTF-8, the other UTF variants UTF-7 and UTF-16 may also be used. The encoding is important since although most users will be using a Latin character encoding, most often English, you can specify a variety of formats to cope with other languages and encoding schemes, for example, the following regional variants can be used:

- ISO-8859-1 Western Europe, USA and South America.
- ISO-8859-2 Central and Eastern Europe.
- ISO-8859-3 South-eastern Europe.
- ISO-8859-4 Scandinavia.
- ISO-8859-5 Cyrillic.
- ISO-8859-3 Arabic.
- ISO-8859-3 Greek.
- ISO-8859-3 Hebrew.
- ISO-8859-3 Turkish.
- ISO-8859-3 Nordic, Eskimo and Lapp.

In addition EUC-JP, Shift_JIS and ISO-2022-JP may be used for Japanese.

If an XML processor does not recognize the encoding type, this is a fatal error and the processing will not proceed.

The *standalone* attribute is optional and can only be assigned to one of two values "yes" or "no". The default is "yes" if it is not included, that is the XML document does not depend on any other XML files to be valid.

The DOCTYPE statement

The DOCTYPE statement specifies a Document Type Definition, (DTD), which defines the elements, attribute names and the relationships between them. A valid document, which the XML processor can understand, conforms to the specified DTD. For example, to define what is valid for the *html* element, the DTD contains the statement:

```
<!ELEMENT html (head, body)>
```

This defines the *html* element as composed of only two elements *head* and *body* (these elements may of course contain other elements).

Definitions are provided for all the elements in the documents, including more complex elements which have detailed attribute lists.

Entities which define the relationship between a group of elements, are defined using an ENTITY declaration, for example:

```
<!ENTITY % heading "H1|H2|H3|H4|H5|H6">
```

Finally items such as image files which are not to be parsed as XML are given using a NOTATION declaration.

```
<!NOTATION gif SYSTEM "image/gif">
```

If you are not going to produce your own definitions you do not need to worry about the format of the DTD - you can simply use one of the three standard ones defined by the W3C. To reference a DTD the DOCTYPE statement must be used.

The DOCTYPE statement has the following five components:

```
<!DOCTYPE html  PUBLIC | SYSTEM  DTDidentifier  URLofDTT
```

1. It must start with an opening <! which indicates it is an XML declaration, followed by the keyword DOCTYPE.
2. The type of document, this must be *html* for XHTML documents.
3. A keyword follows which must be either PUBLIC, indicating that the DTD is publicly available or SYSTEM which indicates that it is not publicly available.
4. The identifier of the DTD is next, for example:

```
"-//W3C//DTD XHTML 1.0 Strict//EN"
```

5. Finally the URL of the DTD, for example

```
"http://www.w3.org/TR/xhtml1/DTD/xhtml1-strict.dtd">
```

An example of a complete statement is shown below:

```
<!DOCTYPE html
PUBLIC "-//W3C//DTD XHTML 1.0 Strict//EN"
"http://www.w3.org/TR/xhtml1/DTD/xhtml1-strict.dtd">
```

If you wish to define your own DTD you should use the SYSTEM keyword and a valid URL. If you want to use a PUBLIC DTD use that keyword and a public identifier. This looks like a URL, but in fact is just a unique string which is recognized by the browser. At the moment, the three public DTDs are hard coded into the browser, but in the future they may be real URLs stored elsewhere which can be downloaded.

The three public DTDs defined by the W3C provide different variants of XHTML:

- Strict. This variant does not allow the use of deprecated elements and attributes. These are features that most browsers will recognize, but there is no guarantee that they will be supported in the future. For example, the elements used for specifying fonts and colours directly rather than by using style sheets. By deprecating an element or attribute, the developer is being given notice not to use them for future documents. The DOCTYPE statement for the Strict DTD is:

```
<!DOCTYPE html
PUBLIC "-//W3C//DTD XHTML 1.0 Strict//EN"
"http://www.w3.org/TR/xhtml1/DTD/xhtml1-strict.dtd">
```

• Transitional. The Transitional DTD supports most of the deprecated elements apart from frames. The DOCTYPE statement for the Transitional DTD is:

```
<!DOCTYPE html
PUBLIC "-//W3C//DTD XHTML 1.0 Transitional//EN"
"http://www.w3.org/TR/xhtml1/DTD/xhtml1-transitional.dtd">
```

• Frameset. This should be used to create a frameset document. The DOCTYPE statement for the Frameset DTD is:

```
<!DOCTYPE html
PUBLIC "-//W3C//DTD XHTML 1.0 Frameset//EN"
"http://www.w3.org/TR/xhtml1/DTD/xhtml1-frameset.dtd">
```

If you are creating documents which may be displayed using older browsers which do not support style sheets, you will need to use the deprecated elements for formatting. Therefore the best DTD to use in these circumstances is the Transitional DTD since it still supports the deprecated elements, however ideally you should use either the Strict or Frameset DTDs. Since the latest browsers can be downloaded free, most people tend not to use old versions.

The namespace declaration

The *<html>* tag must be the first tag in the document. The *xmlns* attribute specifies XML the namespace of the document, for example:

```
<html xmlns = "http://www.w3.org/1999/xhtml">
```

This is the default XML namespace which states that this document uses XHTML.

If the document was another XML document type such as MathML, the DTD and namespace would be different, for example:

```
<?xml version = "1.0" encoding = "UTF-8">
<!DOCTYPE math
PUBLIC "-//W3C//DTD MathML 2.0//EN"
"http://www.w3.org/TR/M<MathML/DTD/mathml2.dtd">
<mm1 xmlns="http://www.w3.org/1998/Math/MathML">
```

In addition to using one of the standard namespaces, you can create your own which allows you to create your own elements and attributes.

The *</html>* tag ends the *html* element and closes the document.

Combining namespaces

You can combine namespaces in the same document. The documents we are going to look at next combine the MathML and the XHTML namespaces.

If you want to see how they appear on your system you will need a browser such as Amaya 6.2 or later, since the most popular browsers, Internet Explorer 6.0 and Netscape 6.2, do not support MathML and the documents will not display correctly. The Amaya browser is designed by the W3C and has facilities that allow it to be used as an authoring tool. Version 6.2 supports MathML, SVG, CSS and HTTP as well as HTML and XHTML. It can be downloaded free.

Figure 3.1 shows a document, in the Amaya browser, which uses the XHTML and MathML namespaces:

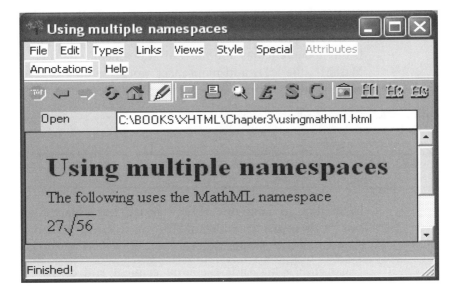

Figure 3.1 *A document with two namespaces.*

The document is shown below:

```
<?xml version="1.0" encoding="ISO-8859-1"?>
<!DOCTYPE html PUBLIC "-//W3C//DTD XHTML 1.0 Strict//EN"
"http://www.w3.org/TR/xhtml1/DTD/xhtml1-strict.dtd">
<html xmlns="http://www.w3.org/1999/xhtml">
<head>
<title>Using multiple namespaces</title>
</head>
<body>
<h1>Using multiple namespaces</h1>
<p>The following uses the MathML namespace</p>
<math xmlns="http://www.w3.org/1998/Math/MathML">
<mn>27</mn>
<msqrt>
<mn>56</mn>
<mo></mo>
</msqrt>
</math>
</body>
</html>
```

The document starts in a normal way, but has a second line namespace declaration:

```
<math xmlns="http://www.w3.org/1998/Math/MathML">
```

This indicates that the following elements are to be interpreted using that namespace.

The closing tag:

```
</math>
```

indicates the end of this namespace and the restoration of the XHTML namespace.

An alternative way of using multiple namespaces is to define the two (or more) namespaces in the *<html>* tag and then to refer to each element of the secondary *math* namespace, preceding them by the name of the namespace. The document below has exactly the same appearance as the previous example:

```
<?xml version="1.0" encoding="ISO-8859-1"?>
<!DOCTYPE html PUBLIC "-//W3C//DTD XHTML 1.0 Strict//EN"
"http://www.w3.org/TR/xhtml1/DTD/xhtml1-strict.dtd">
<html xmlns="http://www.w3.org/1999/xhtml"
      xmlns:math="http://www.w3.org/1998/Math/MathML">
<head>
<title>Using multiple namespaces</title>
</head>
<body>
<h1>Using multiple namespaces version 2</h1>
<p>The following uses the MathML namespace</p>
<math:mn>27</math:mn>
<math:msqrt>
<math:mn>56</math:mn>
<math:mo></math:mo>
</math:msqrt>
</body>
</html>
```

Remember if you try these examples, to use a browser which supports MathML such as Amaya.

Now that we have looked at the xml, DOCTYPE and namespace statements we are ready to write our first XHTML document.

There are a few elements which are either required or are a good idea to include when writing an XHTML document. We are going to look at these.

The html element

The *<html>* and *</html>* tags indicate that the document uses HTML or XHTML. They are required by browsers which do not support the DOCTYPE statement. The opening *<html>* tag should be placed immediately after the DOCTYPE statement. The *</html>* tag should be the last tag in the document, for example:

```
<?xml version = "1.0" encoding = "ISO-8859-1"?>
<!DOCTYPE html PUBLIC "-//W3C//DTD XHTML 1.0 Transitional//EN"
"http://www.w3.org/TR/xhtml1/DTD/xhtml1-transitional.dtd">
<html xmlns = "http://www.w3.org/1999/xhtml">
....
....
</html>
```

White space

It is important when typing tags not to add extra white space, for example the *<head>* tag should be typed:

```
<head>
```

without any spaces. Similarly a closing *</html>* tag should not include any white space. If you do not type the element correctly, the browser will interpret it simply as text and display it.

The one exception to this rule is when you have an empty element, that is a tag which does not have a corresponding closing tag, such as the *<hr>* tag which draws a horizontal line:

```
<hr size = "10" width = "100" align = "left" />
```

There must be a space before the closing /> characters.

The head element

The *<head>* tag is placed after the *<html>* tag and contains information about the whole document, including the title, style, and scripting information. The corresponding closing tag is *</head>*.

```
<?xml version = "1.0" encoding = "ISO-8859-1"?>
<!DOCTYPE html PUBLIC "-//W3C//DTD XHTML 1.0 Transitional//EN"
"http://www.w3.org/TR/xhtml1/DTD/xhtml1-transitional.dtd">
<html xmlns = "http://www.w3.org/1999/xhtml">
<head>
</head>
</html>
```

The following three elements, *title*, *meta* and *base* are placed within the *head* element.

The title element

The *title* element is placed within the head element, that is between the *<head>* and *</head>* tags. The title information is displayed in the browser title bar. If a page is bookmarked, this is the default text which will be used for that bookmark.

```
<?xml version = "1.0" encoding = "ISO-8859-1"?>
<!DOCTYPE html PUBLIC "-//W3C//DTD XHTML 1.0 Transitional//EN"
"http://www.w3.org/TR/xhtml1/DTD/xhtml1-transitional.dtd">
<html xmlns = "http://www.w3.org/1999/xhtml">
<head>
<title>My first XHTML document</title>
</head>
</html>
```

The meta element

The *meta* element is an empty element, that is, it does not have a corresponding closing element.

This element is not mandatory, but is extremely useful if you want accurate information about your document to be collected by search engines, for example:

```
<?xml version = "1.0" encoding = "ISO-8859-1"?>
<!DOCTYPE html PUBLIC "-//W3C//DTD XHTML 1.0 Transitional//EN"
"http://www.w3.org/TR/xhtml1/DTD/xhtml1-transitional.dtd">
<html xmlns = "http://www.w3.org/1999/xhtml">
<head>
<meta name = "author" content = "Joanne Harris" />
<meta name = "keywords" content = "chocolate, fudge, cocoa butter" />
<title>My first XHTML document</title>
</head>
</html>
```

In the example above, a search engine can extract the information that the document author is Joanne Harris and the document is about chocolate, fudge and cocoa butter.

The base element

The *base* element is an empty element that allows you to specify the Uniform Resource Locator (URL) that all relative references use as a base. If you do not use this element, all relative links are based on the document location.

The body element

Figure 3.2 shows a simple Web page which has the *head* and *body* elements. The *head* element contains the *title* element which is the title of the document as displayed on the browser title bar. The *body* element contains all other elements which are displayed by the browser.

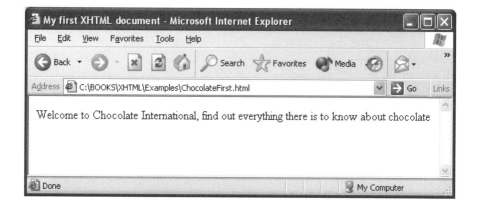

Figure 3.2 The first chocolate Web page.

The XHTML used to produce this page is shown below:

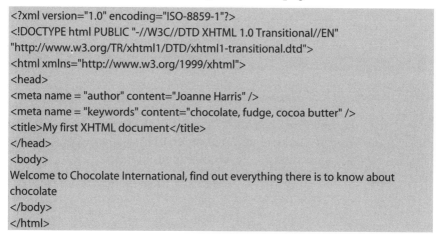

```
<?xml version="1.0" encoding="ISO-8859-1"?>
<!DOCTYPE html PUBLIC "-//W3C//DTD XHTML 1.0 Transitional//EN"
"http://www.w3.org/TR/xhtml1/DTD/xhtml1-transitional.dtd">
<html xmlns="http://www.w3.org/1999/xhtml">
<head>
<meta name = "author" content="Joanne Harris" />
<meta name = "keywords" content="chocolate, fudge, cocoa butter" />
<title>My first XHTML document</title>
</head>
<body>
Welcome to Chocolate International, find out everything there is to know about
chocolate
</body>
</html>
```

Validating the document

If you want to see the web page shown in Figure 3.2, you can download it from the series web site: www.essential-series.com.

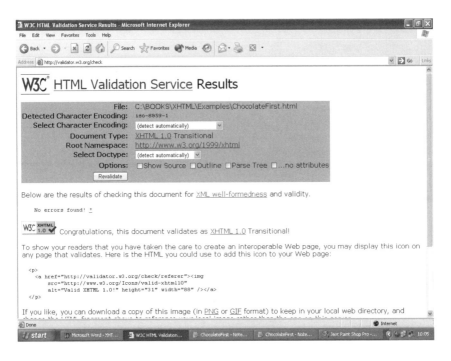

Figure 3.3 *Validating a Transitional XHTML document.*

If, however, you have typed the document yourself, it is easy to make simple typing errors, so it is a good idea to use a validator to pick up these problems.

If you go to the W3C web site http://validator.w3.org/ you can submit an XHTML document and it will be checked for conformity with the standard. Figure 3.3 shows the results of submitting this document.

No errors were found and you may display a small graphic to indicate that this document conforms to the XHTML 1.0 Transitional specification. The document DTD is changed to Strict, by changing the DOCTYPE statement as shown below:

```
<!DOCTYPE html PUBLIC "-//W3C//DTD XHTML 1.0 Strict//EN"
"http://www.w3.org/TR/xhtml1/DTD/xhtml1-strict.dtd">
```

When this document is re-submitted, an error message is produced as shown in Figure 3.4.

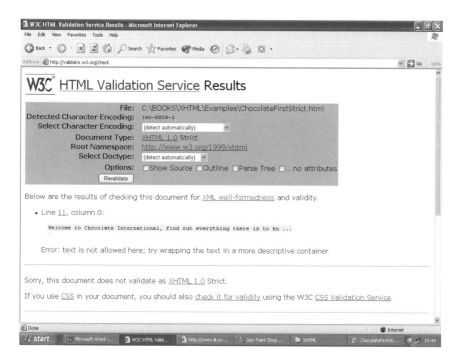

Figure 3.4 *A failed validation.*

The problem is caused by placing text directly within the *body* element without placing it within a formatting element such as the *p* element.

The p element

The *p* element is used to indicate that the text it contains is a single paragraph. New paragraphs begin on a new line and there is usually white space between them. If we place the text within a paragraph, it now conforms to the Strict specification.

```
<body>
<p>
Welcome to Chocolate International, find out everything there is to know about
chocolate
</p>
</body>
```

Unlike most of the other elements we have looked at, you can have as many *p* elements as you wish.

If a paragraph is short you can have the opening and closing tags on the same line:

```
<p>Welcome to Chocolate International</p>
<p>
the place to find out everything there is to know about chocolate
</p>
```

Other paragraph types

In addition to the *p* element, there are two other commonly used paragraph formatting elements (apart from headers):

- *address.* This element is typically used to contain address information. It often appears in italics.
- *pre.* Short for pre-formatted. It is used for showing lines of computer code. It usually has a mono-spaced font with increased line spacing.

An example of using these elements is shown below. Figure 3.5 shows how it is displayed.

```
<?xml version="1.0" encoding="ISO-8859-1"?>
<!DOCTYPE html PUBLIC "-//W3C//DTD XHTML 1.0 Strict//EN"
"http://www.w3.org/TR/xhtml1/DTD/xhtml1-strict.dtd">
<html xmlns="http://www.w3.org/1999/xhtml">
<head>
<title>using p, address and pre elements</title>
</head>
<body>
<p>
A letter to the Times newspaper on the subject of Christmas presents
</p>
<p>
The worst passed-on present my father ever received from his eldest
sister was a pair of what looked like unused bedsocks. He, in fury, gave them to me.
When I put them on I found, a used corn plaster in one of the toe ends. My aunt, at
the time kept a small hotel
</p>
<address>
```

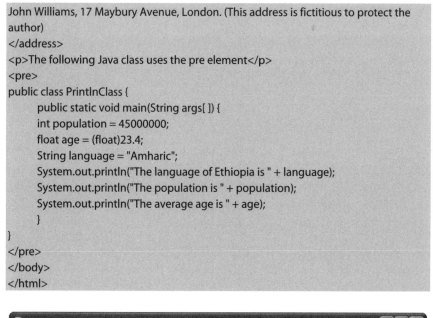

```
John Williams, 17 Maybury Avenue, London. (This address is fictitious to protect the
author)
</address>
<p>The following Java class uses the pre element</p>
<pre>
public class PrintlnClass {
        public static void main(String args[ ]) {
        int population = 45000000;
        float age = (float)23.4;
        String language = "Amharic";
        System.out.println("The language of Ethiopia is " + language);
        System.out.println("The population is " + population);
        System.out.println("The average age is " + age);
        }
}
</pre>
</body>
</html>
```

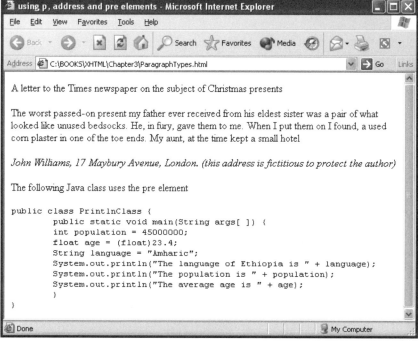

Figure 3.5 Using p, address and pre elements.

Chapter

4

Formatting Documents

Introduction

In the last chapter we looked at how to create a basic XHTML document and display text. In this chapter we are going to look at how to add some formatting to the document to make it easier to read and more attractive. In particular, how to add headings, horizontal lines and lists. We are also going to look briefly at adding colour and specifying the fonts to be used, however these aspects are deprecated in XHTML, that is they are available but not recommended for use. They may not be supported in later versions. The preferred way of controlling those aspects of a document is to use Cascading Style Sheets (CSS), which we look at in Chapter 8.

Headings

A good way to add structure to a document is to use headings. XHTML offers up to six levels of heading, but a document tends to look confusing with more than three levels.

The heading tags are *<h1>*, *<h2>*, *<h3>*, *<h4>*, *<h5>* and *<h6>*, with the corresponding closing tags.

<h1> is the largest heading, the others are sub headings.

An example of these headings is shown below:

```
<?xml version="1.0" encoding="ISO-8859-1"?>
<!DOCTYPE html PUBLIC "-//W3C//DTD XHTML 1.0 Strict//EN"
"http://www.w3.org/TR/xhtml1/DTD/xhtml1-strict.dtd">
<html xmlns="http://www.w3.org/1999/xhtml">
<head>
<title>using heading elements</title>
</head>
<body>
<h1>Level 1 heading</h1>
<h2>Level 2 heading</h2>
<h3>Level 3 heading</h3>
```

```
<h4>Level 4 heading</h4>
<h5>Level 5 heading</h5>
<h6>Level 6 heading</h6>
</body>
</html>
```

The browser produces the page shown in Figure 4.1.

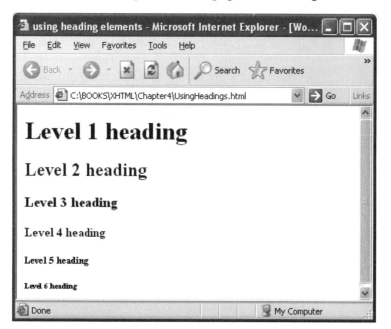

Figure 4.1 Using different headings.

Later examples assume that the XHTML statements are placed in the body of the XHTML document with a preceding xml, DOCTYPE and namespace declaration. This is not shown in every example since it is the same every time.

Line breaks

Sometimes it is useful to say exactly where you want a line break to go. The empty *br* element does this, for example:

```
<p>This is the first line<br />and this is the second</p>
```

Inserting lines

A good way of breaking documents into sections is to use horizontal lines. The empty *hr* element does this.

There are four attributes for this element, however all are deprecated and therefore do not conform to the Strict specification.   However if you are going to use the Transitional form of XHTML they may be used.   In the Strict model, all formatting of documents should be done using style sheets.   The attributes are:

- *align* = "*center*"|"*left*"|"*right*". This aligns the horizontal to the specified position in the browser.
- *noshade* = "*noshade*".   This attribute determines whether the line is shaded or not.
- *size* = "n". The thickness of the line in pixels.
- *width* = "n" | "n%". The length of line in pixels or as a percentage of the width of the document.

An example of using this element and some of its attributes is shown in Figure 4.2.

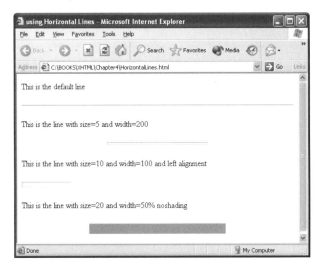

Figure 4.2 Using horizontal lines.

The XHTML used to produce this page is shown below:

```
<head>
<title>using Horizontal Lines</title>
</head>
<body>
<p> This is the default line</p>
<hr />
<p> This is the line with size=5 and width=200 </p>
<hr size="5" width="200"/>
<p> This is the line with size=10 and width=100 and left alignment </p>
<hr size="10" width="100" align="left" />
<p> This is the line with size=20 and width=50% noshading</p>
<hr size="20" width="50%" noshade="noshade" />
</body>
</html>
```

The browser displays this document as shown in Figure 4.2. The document will pass the W3C validation with the Transitional DTD but not with the Strict DTD because some deprecated attributes are used. Note that placing the *hr* element within a paragraph element such as *p* or *pre* causes a validation error.

Colours and Fonts

The XHTML Strict specification deprecates the use of the attributes for controlling colour and fonts in favour of using Cascading Style Sheets (CSS). However, since these attributes are very widely used, a brief review is given here, but they should be avoided where possible.

Colours are specified using the Red, Green, Blue (RGB) model. Each of these three components of the colour must be specified by a hexadecimal number between 0 and FF, that is 0 and 255 decimal.

Setting the background colour

To set the background colour of the document to red, you can use the deprecated attribute *bgcolor* of the *body* element:

```
<body bgcolor = "#FF0000">
```

The red component is specified by the FF part of the hexadecimal number, the green and blue components by the following pairs of zeros.

Since you do not know the capabilities of the screen which will display the document it is advisable to limit the colours to web safe colours by assigning each of the three components to either 00, 33, 66, 99, CC, or FF. For example, #33FF66, gives a colour which is predominately green with a little blue and even less red.

Setting the text colour

You can assign different colours to different parts of the text using a set of four deprecated attributes of the *body* element:

- *text*. Assigns the colour to all text (apart from the links where a different colour may be specified).
- *link*. Links which have not been visited yet.
- *alink*. Active links, that is links which the user is clicking.
- *vlink*. Visited links.

The example below shows these attributes in use:

```
<body text = "#000000" link = "#00FF00" alink = "#0000FF" vlink = "#33CC99">
```

Setting the font

The font used can be specified by the deprecated *font* element.

The *font* element has four deprecated attributes:

- *color*. The colour of the text, as specified using a hexadecimal number.
- *face*. The font to be used. A list may be given in order of precedence.
- *size*. A value between 1 and 7. 1 is the smallest. The default is 3. A relative size can be specified by writing, for example, +1.
- *basefont*. The default font for the document.

An example of using this element and its attributes is shown below.

```
<font color = "#6633CC" face = "Helvetica, Arial, Myriad" size = "+1">
Hello everyone
</font>
```

Lists

It is often useful to add lists to your document, and XHTML offers a variety of options. You can have: numbered lists which start from any specified number; unnumbered lists which use a specified bullet type.

To create a list:

- Enclose the list items between a *<ol>* and *</ol>* pair of tags for a numbered (ordered) list and the *<ul>* and *</ul>* tag pair for a bulleted (unordered) list.
- Place each list item within an *<li> </li>* pair.

The example below produces the bulleted list shown on the left of Figure 4.3:

```
<head>
<title>Chocolate 'facts'</title>
```

```
</head>
<body>
<p>
Chocolate is good for you because:
</p>
<ul>
<li>It tastes great.</li>
<li>It's rich in anti-oxidants.</li>
<li>It gives a sense of well-being.</li>
<li>it raises your blood sugar level.</li>
</ul>
</body>
</html>
```

To produce the numbered list shown on the right of Figure 4.3 simply substitute the *<ol>* and *</ol>* tags for the *<ul>* and *</ul>* tags.

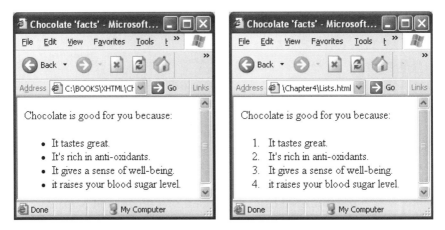

Figure 4.3 Displaying lists.

If you want you can change the bullet which is displayed in unordered lists by using the *type* attribute, which may be assigned the values *disc*, *square* or *circle*, for example:

```
<ul type = "square">
```

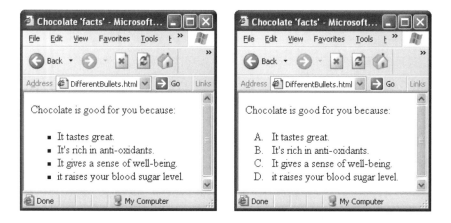

Figure 4.4 *Changing bullets and numbering systems.*

The picture on the left of Figure 4.4 shows square bullets.

You can also change the numbering system used by the numbered list from 1,2,3. You can specify A, a, I, i, or the default of 1. An example is shown below:

```
<ol type = "A">
```

The result of using this attribute is shown on the right of Figure 4.4. If you wish, you can specify the starting value for a numbered list by using the *value* parameter, for example:

```
<ol type = "a" value = "3">
```

This will start a numbered list at c, the third lower case letter of the alphabet.

Nesting lists

Sometimes you may want to include a sub-list within another list. This is straightforward to do using the elements we have already seen. The code below gives an example of this.

```
<ol type = "i">
<li>It tastes great.</li>
     <ul type = "disc">
          <li>it's creamy.</li>
          <li>it's sweet.</li>
          <li>it's rich.</li>
     </ul>
<li>It's rich in anti-oxidants.</li>
<li>It gives a sense of well-being.</li>
<li>it raises your blood sugar level.</li>
</ol>
```

The document as displayed by the browser is shown in Figure 4.5.

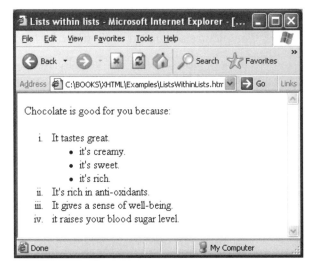

Figure 4.5 *Lists with lists.*

Definition lists

The final form of lists we are going to look at are definition lists using the *dl* and *dt* elements. As the name suggests, these are usually used to provide a glossary of terms, for example, the statements listed below list a few of the wedding presents given to Princess Anne and Captain Mark Philips. Figure 4.6 shows how this document is displayed in the browser.

```
<head>
<title>Definition Lists</title>
</head>
<body>
<p>
A few items from the published List of Wedding Presents to Princess Anne and Captain
Mark Philips (this is true!)
</p>
<dl>
<dt>Tadeusz Rogala.</dt>
<dd>Book, Sewers of Warsaw.</dd>
<dt>Mr. F. Pella</dt>
<dd>Various carvings out of coal.</dd>
<dt>Rev. Canon and Mrs. C.L. Condor</dt>
<dd>Three felt mice.</dd>
</dl>
</body>
</html>
```

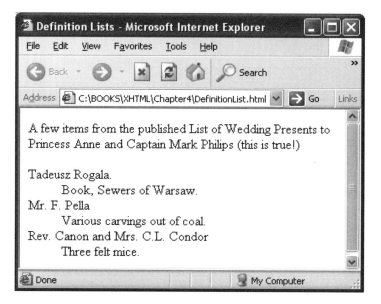

Figure 4.6 *Definition lists.*

Chapter 5

Creating Links

Introduction

One of the most important aspects of XHTML documents is that you can move to another document or another place in the same document by clicking on a link. Links are straightforward to create and you do not have to worry about how the link is displayed – the browser does that for you. In this chapter we are going to look at:

- What is a URL?
- Using absolute URLs.
- Using relative URLs.
- Links within a document.

What is a URL?

URL is short for Uniform Resource Locator. It identifies a new document or place in the current document that can be displayed by a browser. A URL consists of four components:

- A protocol identifier.
- The name of the Web server.
- The name of the folder on the Web server.
- The name of the file.

For example, in the URL shown in Figure 5.1:

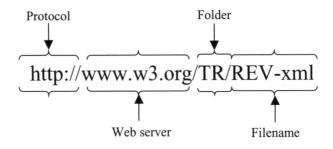

Figure 5.1 The format of a URL.

It is assumed that the file name has an extension of htm or html.

The protocol identifier

A protocol specifies the format in which data is stored. This will be different if you are downloading a document from a Web server or opening a local file on your computer.

The most common protocol you will use is *http://*, this indicates that the document is located on a Web and usually that it is an XHTML or HTML document.

If you are reading a file from your own computer specify *file:///*, note the third slash in place of the name of the Web server.

ftp:// indicates a document on an ftp (file transfer protocol) server.

mailto: is not standard, but is widely supported. It is used to open an email system to send a message to the specified address. Other protocols less commonly used include *gopher://* and *telnet://*

The Web server

This is the name of the Web server which holds the document you wish to reference.

The folder and filename

The folder (or directory) and filename gives the full pathname of the file you are linking to. Sometimes you can omit the filename if you wish to display the default home page. An extension on .htm or .html is implied and so you do not need to specify this.

The a element

To insert a link, you use the *<a> </a>* pair, (the *a* stands for anchor, another name for a link). Within this element you use the *href* attribute which specifies the address, for example:

```
<a href = "http://www.essential-series/index.html">Essential series home page</a>
```

The text *Essential series home page* is the text which is displayed as a link in the document. Clicking on this text moves to that document.

Absolute and relative URLs

There are two types of URLs, absolute and relative. If you want to link to a document on another server you must specify its absolute URL, that is its full address. If you want to refer to a document on the same server or to somewhere in the same document you can use a relative address. The advantage of using a relative address is that if you change your Web site to a new server or to a different location on the same server, all of these links will still work, providing that their relative addresses remain the same.

Absolute URLs

Absolute URLs are the most straightforward to use, they consist of the full list of required items: the protocol, the web server, the folder and the file name. If you want to link to another Web site you should use an absolute URL, for example:

```
<a href = "http://www.essential-series.com/">Essential series home page</a>
<br />
<a href = "http://www.iii.co.uk">interactive investor</a>
<br />
<a href = "http://www.google.com/">google</a>
```

```
<br />
<a href = "ftp://ftp.w3.org/pub/">W3c </a>
```

Relative URLs

A relative URL is used when you want to provide a link to a document on the same server or to a location in the same document.

To link to a document on the same server and the same folder you can just specify the filename – without the protocol, Web server and folder.

To link to a document on the same server which is in a different folder you must give both the folder and the filename.

Figure 5.2 shows a set of XHTML files stored on a web server. The top level folder contains a single file called *index* and two folders called *chocolatenews* and *chocolatestores*. The *chocolatenews* folder contains a single folder called *archive*.

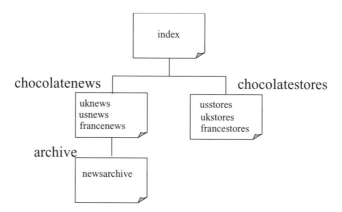

Figure 5.2 *Using relative addressing.*

We are going to look at how you can link between all of the following files: *index, uknews, usstores* and *newsarchive*.

If you want to try this example on your computer you will need to create the folder structure and the files (remember the html extension) on your computer.

To link from *index.html* to the other three files the following links are needed:

```
<a href = "chocolatenews/uknews.html">to uknews</a>
<a href = "chocolatenews/archive/newsarchive.html">to newsarchive</a>
<a href = "chocolatestores/usstores.html">to usstores</a>
```

- In the first link the file *uknews.html* is in the subfolder called *chocolatenews*.
- Since the file *newsarchive.html* is in a sub-folder of *chocolatenews* called *archive*, this must be specified.
- The third link is to the file *usstores* which is in a folder called *chocolatestores*.

To link from the file *uknews* in the *chocolatenews* subfolder, to the other three files the following links are required:

```
<a href = "../index.html">to index</a>
<a href = "../chocolatestores/usstores.html">to usstores</a>
<a href = "archive/newsarchive.html">to newsarchive</a>
```

To link to *index.html*, which is above the *chocolatenews* folder containing the *uknews* file, a new notation is used. The ../ means that you should move upwards to the parent folder.

To move to the *usstores.html* file, we must first move up to the parent directory (hence ../) then move down to the *chocolatestores* folder.

To specify the *newsarchive.html* file which is in the archive sub-folder you need only specify the name of the archive folder.

In a similar way the links from the *usstores.html* file are:

```
<a href = "../index.html">back to index</a>
<a href = "../chocolateNews/uknews.html">to uknews</a>
<a href = "../chocolateNews/archive/newsarchive.html">to newsarchive</a>
```

and the links from the *newsarchive.html* file are:

```
<a href = ".. /../index.html">to index</a>
<a href = "../../chocolatestores/usstores.html">to usstores</a>
<a href = "../uknews.html">to uknews</a>
```

Note that to reach the *index.html* file we must move up two levels, two ../ pairs are required.

Server relative URLs

Sometimes it is useful to be able to add a link which is relative to the root of the server rather than to the current location of the document. The syntax for doing this is to add a single / character at the start of the URL, for example to reference the file *index.html* from any document in any location on the server you could add the link:

```
<a href = "/index.html">a link to the index page</a>
```

This simplifies out document references from the previous example, for example to reference the *usstores.html* file from the *newsarchive.html* file instead of typing:

```
<a href = "../../chocolatestores/usstores.html">to usstores</a>
```

we can type:

```
<a href = "/chocolatestores/usstores.html">to usstores</a>
```

The first / character indicates that the following location is relative to the server root.

Links within a document

Sometimes it is useful to provide a document which has an index at the start and links to other parts of the document. There is a straightforward syntax for doing this. There are two parts to setting up internal links: firstly the point you want to link to must be specified; secondly the link must be created.

To create the point you are linking to, the *a* element is used with the *name* attribute, for example:

```
<a name = "Miami">Miami chocolate stores</a>
```

The name of the link is *Miami*, the text *Miami chocolate stores* appears as normal text in the document, that is, it does not appear as a link.

To link to this point from the same document:

```
<a href = "#Miami">Miami stores</a>
```

Note the # character in front of the link name. If you want to point to this place from another document, you can do so in the usual way, for example:

```
<a href = "chocolatestores/usstores.html#Miami">Miami stores</a>
```

The name of the link, including the # is specified as before.

Email links

It can be very useful to add a link which creates an empty email with a specified address

```
<a href ="mailto:bill@breakawayflyingschool.com">Email us<a>
```

Clicking on this link will run the user's default email application.

This is not a part of the XHTML standard, but it is supported by most browsers.

Chapter 6

Creating and Using Tables

Introduction

Tables are an excellent way of displaying information each within its own grid cell. You can even use a table with two or more columns and one row to display text in columns.

Tables have been a source of difficulty in HTML with different browsers supporting different formatting attributes. In XHTML many attributes have been deprecated in favour of style sheets, however they are still supported and are very widely used, so we are going to look at the key ones.

In this chapter we are going to look at how to:

- Create tables.
- Control column and row size.
- Span across more than one column.
- Control border appearance.

Creating tables

Some types of information are most clearly displayed in a table, an example is shown in Figure 6.1, which displays the chocolate consumption per year for various countries.

A table is made up of a set of rows; each row is made up of individual cells, each of which contains some text. To create a table you need the following elements:

- The *caption* element provides a title for the whole table.
- The *<table>* tag and the corresponding closing *</table>* tag, which enclose all the information on the table.
- The *tr* element defines a row in the table.
- The *th* element is used to define a table heading.
- The *td* element defines an individual cell.

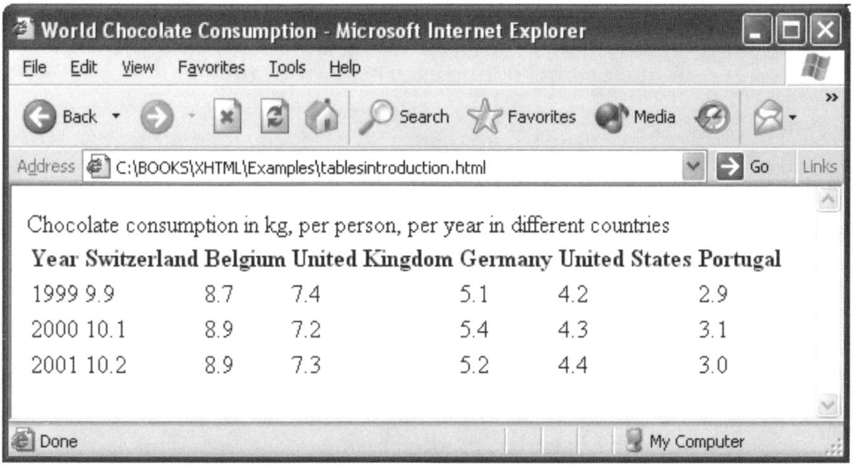

Figure 6.1 Using a table to display world chocolate consumption.

To define the table shown in Figure 6.1, first add the opening *<table>* tag:

```
<table>
```

Next the optional *caption* element

```
<caption>
Chocolate consumption in kg, per person, per year in different countries
</caption>
```

This element is optional, you do not need to include it if you do not wish to add a title to the table.

Specify a row using the *<tr>* tag and place the header elements between it and the closing *</tr>* tag.

```
<tr>
<th>Year</th>
<th>Switzerland</th>
<th>Belgium</th>
<th>United Kingdom</th>
<th>Germany</th>
<th>United States</th>
<th>Portugal</th>
</tr>
```

Finally add each row by starting with the *<tr>* tag. A series of *td* elements define each cell, for example:

```
<tr>
<td>1999</td>
<td>9.9</td>
<td>8.7</td>
<td>7.4</td>
<td>5.1</td>
<td>4.2</td>
<td>2.9</td>
</tr>
```

The row is ended by the closing *</tr>* tag. This is repeated for each row in the table. The completed body of the document is shown below:

```
<head>
<title>World Chocolate Consumption</title>
</head>
<body>
<table>
<caption>
Chocolate consumption in kg, per person, per year in different countries
</caption>
<tr>
<th>Year</th>
<th>Switzerland</th>
<th>Belgium</th>
<th>United Kingdom</th>
<th>Germany</th>
<th>United States</th>
<th>Portugal</th>
</tr>
<tr>
<td>1999</td>
<td>9.9</td>
<td>8.7</td>
<td>7.4</td>
<td>5.1</td>
<td>4.2</td>
<td>2.9</td>
</tr>
```

```
<tr>
<td>2000</td>
<td>10.1</td>
<td>8.9</td>
<td>7.2</td>
<td>5.4</td>
<td>4.3</td>
<td>3.1</td>
</tr>
<tr>
<td>2001</td>
<td>10.2</td>
<td>8.9</td>
<td>7.3</td>
<td>5.2</td>
<td>4.4</td>
<td>3.0</td>
</tr>
</table>
</body>
</html>
```

Formatting tables

The appearance of a table can be greatly changed by adding a border to the cells. This is done using the *border* attribute, for example:

```
<table border = "2">
```

Changing the *<table>* tag as shown above in the previous example produces the table shown in Figure 6.2.

If the value of the *border* attribute is "0" there is no visible border. This is the default. The larger the value, the thicker the border.

XHTML introduces some extra formatting options over HTML which allow you to only display certain borders, by using the *frame* and *rules* attributes of the *table* element.

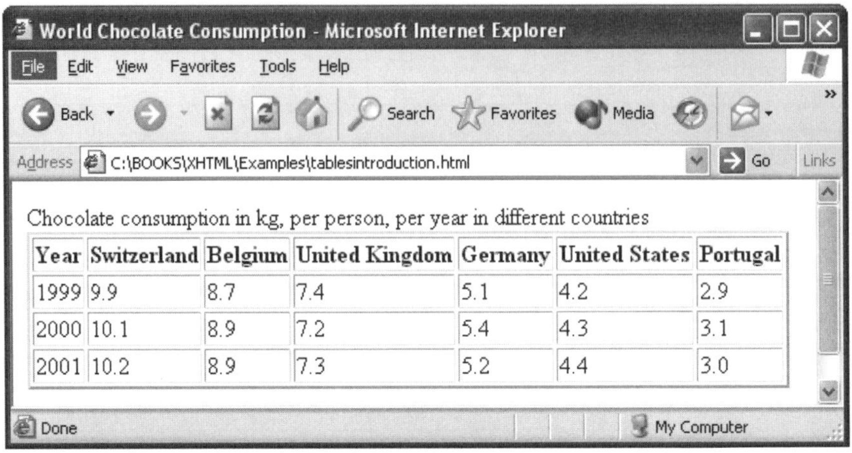
World Chocolate Consumption - Microsoft Internet Explorer
File Edit View Favorites Tools Help
Back Search Favorites Media
Address C:\BOOKS\XHTML\Examples\tablesintroduction.html Go Links
Chocolate consumption in kg, per person, per year in different countries
Year Switzerland Belgium United Kingdom Germany United States Portugal
1999 9.9 8.7 7.4 5.1 4.2 2.9
2000 10.1 8.9 7.2 5.4 4.3 3.1
2001 10.2 8.9 7.3 5.2 4.4 3.0
Done My Computer

Figure 6.2 *Adding a border to cells.*

The *frame* attribute can have the values shown in Table 6.1:

Table 6.1 Values of the *frame* attribute.

Value	Meaning
void	No border.
above	A border at the top of the table.
below	A border at the bottom of the table.
border	A border around every cell.
hsides	A border along the top and bottom.
lhs	A border on the left edge.
rhs	A border on the right edge.
vsides	A border on both the left and right.

This attribute should be used in conjunction with the *rules* attribute. This can have the values shown in Table 6.2.

Figure 6.3 is created by using these values for the *frame* and *rules* attributes:

```
<table border="2" frame ="hsides" rules ="none">
```

Table 6.2 Values of the *rules* attribute.

Value	Meaning
none	No internal lines.
rows	Horizontal lines between rows.
cols	Vertical lines between columns.
all	Boxes around all cells.
groups	Rules between groups as defined by the thead, tfoot and tbody elements.

Figure 6.4 is created by using these values:

```
<table border="3" frame = "box" rules = "cols">
```

It can be difficult to get exactly the effect you want, so it is worthwhile drawing the table on paper and working out the attribute values before starting the coding.

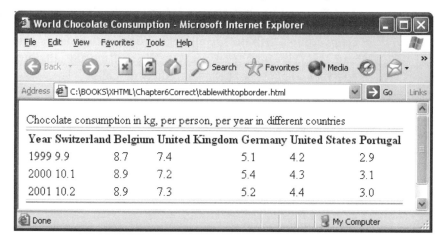

Figure 6.3 Adding a top border to cells.

The *align* attribute for a table is deprecated, and should be avoided wherever possible, however it is still supported by most browsers. For example, to centre the table horizontally in the browser:

```
<table align = "center">
```

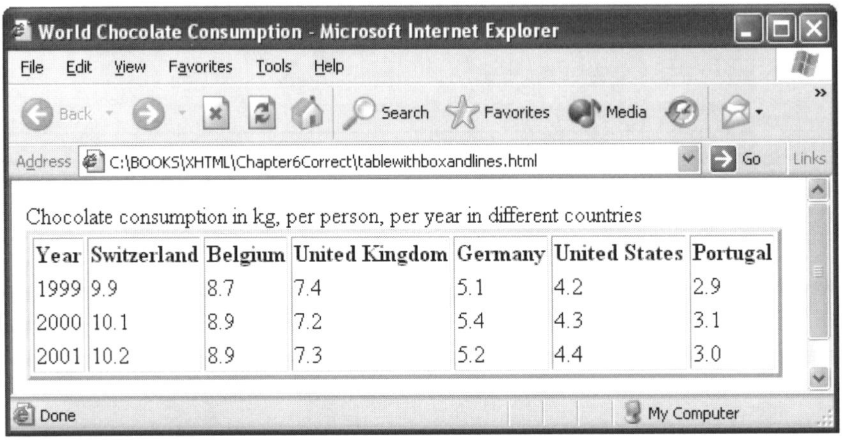

Figure 6.4 Adding a box and vertical lines.

The *cellpadding* and *cellspacing* attributes have a similar function and it is a common mistake to confuse them. The *cellpadding* attribute specifies the edge of the table's cells and the cell content in pixels. The *cellspacing* attribute specifies the space between adjacent cells. These two attributes interact to control the table's appearance.

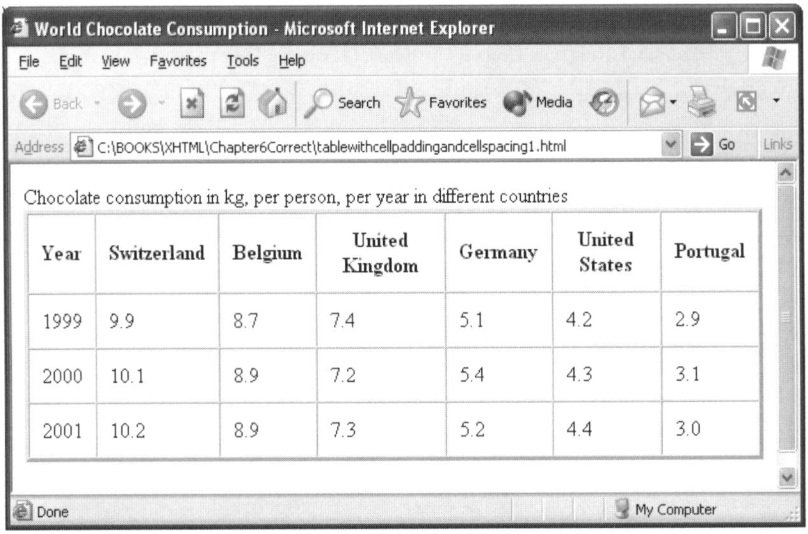

Figure 6.5 Using cellpadding.

Two examples are shown in Figures 6.5 and 6.6.

The table in Figure 6.5 is created by using these values:

```
<table border="3" cellpadding="10" cellspacing="0">
```

The table in Figure 6.6 is created by using these values:

```
<table border = "3" cellpadding = "5" cellspacing = "10">
```

There are numerous other formatting attributes for controlling colours that you may come across, which are deprecated, but still recognized by browsers, for example:

- *bordercolor* = "00FF00", this makes the border green.
- *bgcolor* = "0000FF", this makes the background colour blue.
- *background* = "nicepic.gif", this tiles the specified graphics file onto the table background.

These attributes still work with the most popular browsers, but should not be used if possible – the preferred method in XHTML is to use style sheets. 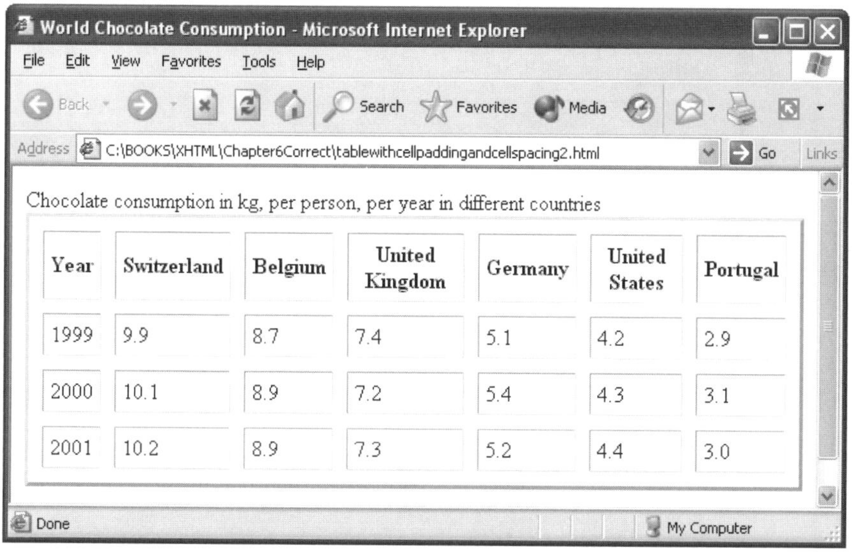

Figure 6.6 Using cellpadding and cellspacing.

Formatting cells

The attributes we have looked at control the appearance of the whole table, but you can control the appearance of individual cells, by specifying a range of attributes for the *<tr>* and *<td>* tags.

The align and valign attributes

The *align* attribute can be set to either *left, right, center,* or *justify*. The default is *left*. The significance of changing this attribute, for example to center, controls the position of the cell content.

If the *align* attribute is set for a row, that is a *<tr>* tag, the attribute value applies to all of the cells in that row. You can set this attribute for a single cell, using the *<td>* tag. If you set the attribute to a different value for a cell it overrides the value set for the row. For example, to set the alignment for a whole row:

```
<tr align = "center">
```

To set the alignment for a single cell:

```
<td align = "left">
```

This attribute can be assigned the values: *left, right, center, justify* or *char*. The meanings of these is as indicated by the name except for *char* which allows you to line up a specified character such as a decimal point (the default) when a row contains numbers, for example:

```
<td align = "char">8.7</td>
```

Some browsers allow you to extend this and allow you to line up another character, for example to line up commas:

```
<td align = "char" char = ",">8,237</td>
```

The default character, if none is specified, is a period. Support for this is not guaranteed and you should not use it unless you are certain it will be supported by the environment it is to be used in.

The *valign* attribute controls vertical alignment in a row or cell. This can be either: *top, middle, bottom* or *baseline*.

The colspan and rowspan attributes

When a cell is spanned it stretches across more than one row or column. The *colspan* and *rowspan* attributes of the *<td>* tag specify this. In our table which displays chocolate consumption you may wish to add a heading which spans across all of the columns in the table. You can do this by adding the elements shown below, before the row which lists the countries as shown in Figure 6.7.

```
<tr align="center">
<th colspan="4">Countries</th>
</tr>
```

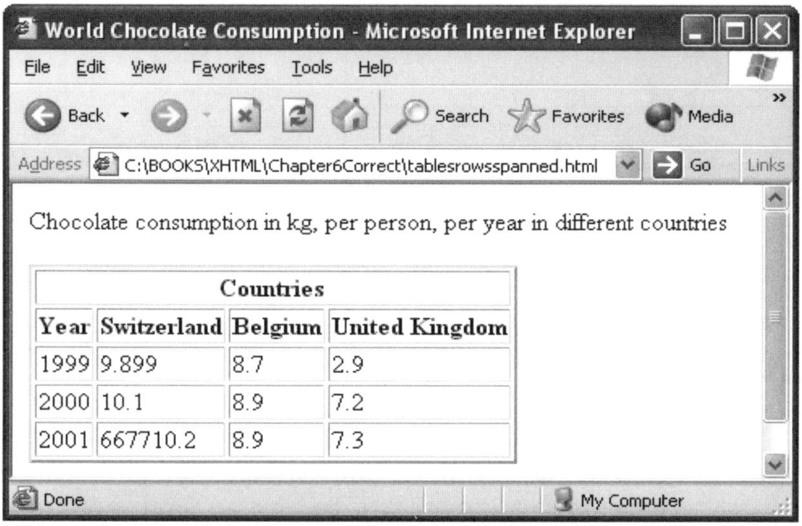

Figure 6.7 Grouping columns.

The appearance can be further improved by spanning the *Year* heading, so that it spans two rows. This item is moved to the position shown below:

```
<tr>
<th rowspan="2">Year</th>
<th colspan="4">Countries</th>
</tr>
```

The resulting table is shown in Figure 6.8.

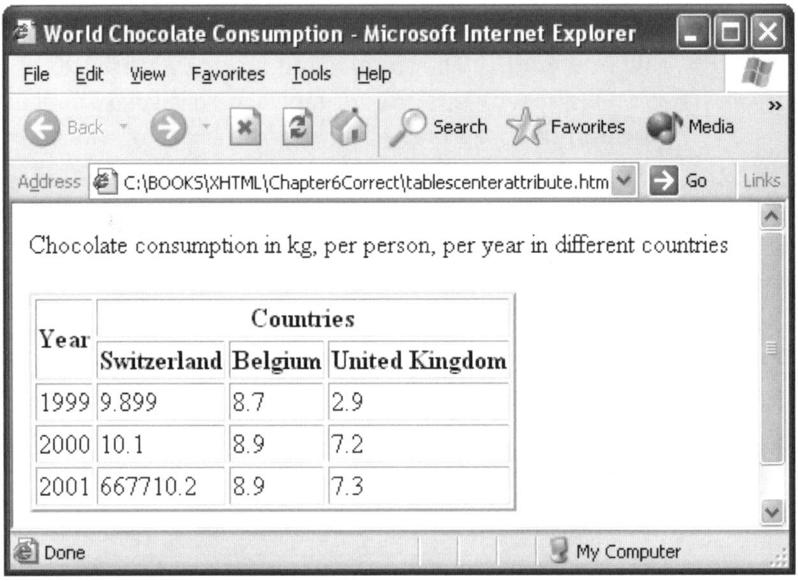

Figure 6.8 *Grouping rows and columns.*

Grouping table elements

The formatting options we have looked at so far have either been applied to the entire table, a row or a cell, but sometimes it is useful to be able to label the different regions of the table. These regions may be addressed individually and given different characteristics, for example, you may want the header to be in a different colour to the body. This labelling can be done using the *thead*, *tfoot* and *tbody* elements, within the *table* element:

- The *<thead>* and *</thead>* pair enclose the part of the table which defines the header.
- The *<tfoot>* and *</tfoot>* pair encloses a footer to the table. Sometimes the header may be repeated as a footer to enable it to be read more easily – particularly if the table contains many rows.
- The *<tbody>* and *</tbody>* pair enclose the main body of the table.

These three elements must be used in this order after the opening *<table>* tag:

```
<table border = "2">
```

The *<thead>* tag is next:

```
<thead>
<tr>
     <th>Year</th>
     <th>Switzerland</th>
     <th>Belgium</th>
     <th>United Kingdom</th>
</tr>
</thead>
```

The footer part follows:

```
<tfoot>
<tr>
<td>Year</td>
<td>Switzerland</td>
<td>Belgium</td>
<td>United Kingdom</td>
</tr>
</tfoot>
```

Finally the body:

```
<tbody>
<tr>
<td>1999</td> <td>9.8</td>
<td>8.7</td> <td>2.9</td>
```

```
</tr>
<tr>
<td>2000</td> <td>10.1</td>
<td>8.9</td> <td>7.2</td>
</tr>
<tr>
<td>2001</td> <td>10.2</td>
<td>8.9</td> <td>7.3</td>
</tr>
</tbody>
```

The closing *</table>* tag ends the table.

```
</table>
```

This effect of labelling these regions has no impact on the appearance of the document, shown in Figure 6.9, but allows them to be handled differently by a style sheet.

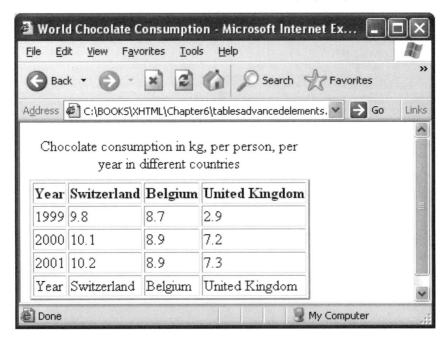

Figure 6.9 *Labelling parts of a table.*

The colgroup element

In addition, you can identify a column group within a table, or columns within a column group using the *colgroup* element.

The *colgroup* elements should be placed at the start of the table as shown below:

```
<caption>
Chocolate consumption in kg, per person, per year in different countries
</caption>
<table border="2">
<colgroup span="1" bgcolor ="EEEEEE" ></colgroup>
<colgroup span="6" bgcolor ="BBBBBB"></colgroup>
```

This creates two groups, the first has just one column and the second six columns. The deprecated attributes are used to give each of these column groups a distinctive background colour. They appear correctly in most browsers, but to pass the W3C validation you will need to remove the *bgcolor* attributes.

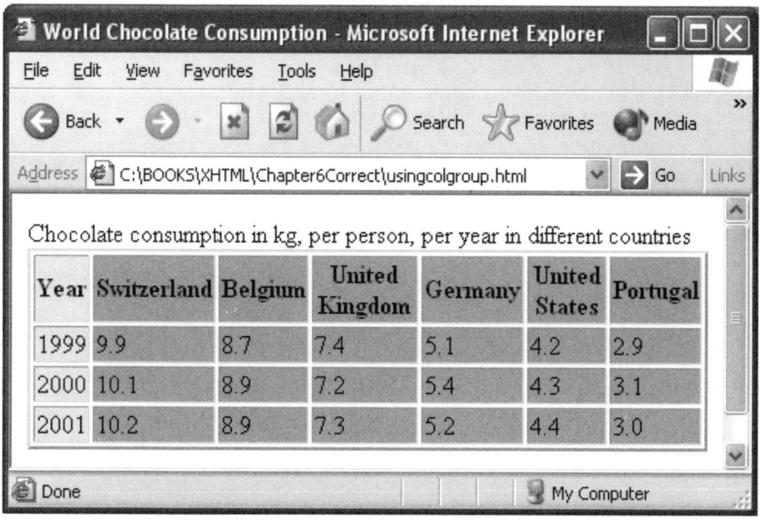

Year	Switzerland	Belgium	United Kingdom	Germany	United States	Portugal
1999	9.9	8.7	7.4	5.1	4.2	2.9
2000	10.1	8.9	7.2	5.4	4.3	3.1
2001	10.2	8.9	7.3	5.2	4.4	3.0

Figure 6.10 Using column groups.

Figure 6.10 is the same table as Figure 6.2, apart from the different colouring of the two column groups.

Style sheets

We have looked at how to control many of the key aspects of table appearance, but there are some other features which we have not dealt with, such as controlling the width of the table or its position on the page. These aspects are controlled by attributes which are deprecated. The preferred way of controlling them is by using style sheets. If you want to write XHTML documents which will be supported by later versions of browsers you should avoid deprecated elements wherever possible.

Chapter
7

Working with Images

Introduction

Images can be used to give information, for example a map, or a picture of a product you may wish to buy, or simply to make a page more attractive. The only problem with images is that they are much larger than text and can take a long time to download. If a page is not displayed in a few seconds, people go elsewhere. More people are using high speed broadband services, but the majority of internet users are still using modems with a speed of 56Kbps or less, so you need to bear this in mind when deciding what images to add to your pages.

In this chapter we are going to look at:

- Image formats.
- Adding images to a page.
- Using image maps, so that different parts of the same image can be used as links.

Image Formats

The format of an image is the way in which the image information is stored in a file, three formats are used and are supported by all recent browsers:

- GIF. Graphics Interchange Format.
- JPEG. Joint Photographic Experts Group.
- PNG. Portable Network Graphics.

Each of these formats has its own set of strengths and weaknesses and should be used in different circumstances.

GIF files

GIF files can have up to 256 different colours, if your image has less colours than this, many image editing applications such as Paint Shop Pro allow you specify the number of colours, between 3 and 256. This reduces the file size. There are two versions of this format which are still supported by most applications, 87a and 89a. The latest version is 89a and it is best to use this format. GIF uses a form of compression which is called lossless which means that an image stored in GIF does not lose information, in contrast to JPEG which uses lossy compression, which can cause a loss of information particularly with files which have large expanses of the same colour.

A useful feature of GIF format files is that you can make a background transparent, so that it is not surrounded by a box. Figure 7.1 shows the same picture – the image on the left has a transparent background while the one on the right does not.

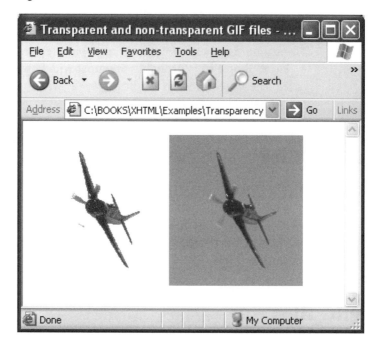

Figure 7.1 *Transparent and non-transparent GIF files.*

You can achieve the same effect by making the background colour of your page the same as the background colour of the image, but unless you use a simple colour such as black or white it can be difficult to achieve an exact match.

GIF files can be interlaced, so that instead of the image appearing line by line, every eighth line is displayed until the entire image is displayed, although it takes the same time for the whole image to be downloaded, the viewer sees the image becoming clearer. It is usually possible to see what the image is like before the whole of it has been displayed.

A useful feature of GIF files is that you can use animated GIFs to add movement to your page. Animated GIF files can be large since the file contains a series of images which are displayed consecutively.

Most recent image editing and creation applications provide an excellent set of tools for saving GIF files with varying numbers of colours, transparency and interlacing. Paint Shop Pro is probably the most widely used which has all these features in addition to a wizard for creating animated GIF files.

JPEG files

The main advantage of JPEG over GIF is that JPEG supports millions of colours rather than the maximum of 256 in GIF. It also supports interlacing, but does not support transparency or animation. It uses lossy compression.

PNG files

PNG is a more recent file format and combines the advantages of GIF and JPEG, it supports millions of colours, interlacing, transparency and animation. It uses lossless compression. The size of PNG files tends to be greater than GIF files but less than JPEG files, although this depends on the image. Recent versions of image editing applications support this format.

PNG is supported by the latest browsers, although if you want your pages to be viewable by the greatest number of users, choose one of the other two formats.

Which format should I use?

JPEG is the most suitable format for photographic images where the loss of resolution caused by lossy compression is less noticeable, and the largest number of colours are required.

GIF files should be used for line drawings where the number of colours is limited.

If you know your target viewers will have up-to-date browsers use PNG, however it is always worthwhile checking the file size in the other two formats and seeing if the images in those formats are acceptable.

Minimizing file size

One of the most important aspects of designing your image files is to ensure that they have the minimum size while still appearing to be clear to the viewer. Most screens have a resolution of 1024×768, so an image that size will fill the entire screen. If you display a large image and reduce the size at which it is shown, the file will still take as long to download, so if an image is larger than you need, use the resize option in your image editing application to reduce it to the required size rather than adjusting its display size in XHTML.

Do not use large animated GIF images. If the file has ten images, the file will be at least ten times the size of a single image of the same size and resolution.

You can work out roughly how long a page will take to download by dividing the size of the page by the speed of the modem. The only complication is that the speed of modems is given in terms of Kilobits (Kb) per second and file size is given in Kilobytes (KB). For example a modem which is rated at 56Kb per second, will download 56/8 = 7 KB per second (since there are 8 bits in a byte). This means that a fairly small 28KB page will take 28/7 = 4 seconds to download with a 56Kb modem. A modem which is rated at 28Kb per second will take twice as long.

Web users are often impatient and if your page takes more than 5 seconds to view, they may go elsewhere.

Displaying images

There is no difference in the XHTML statements, whichever of the image formats you choose.

The *img* element is used to specify the image to be displayed. It has a number of attributes that give the name of the image file and details of how it is to be displayed.

The simplest form of this element requires two attributes to specify the name of the image file and some text which is displayed if users have text only browsers. For example:

```
<img src="transparent.gif" alt="transparent GIF" />
```

The *src* attribute allows the name of the file to be specified. In this case the file is in the same folder as the page it is displayed in. If you wish you can specify a full URL. The *alt* attribute gives some alternative text which is displayed if the image cannot be displayed, if for example the file does not exist.

The *height* and *width* attributes are used to determine the size at which the image is displayed, for example:

```
<img src="transparent.gif" alt="transparent GIF" height="100" width="100" />
```

There are many other attributes which have been deprecated in XHTML in favour of using style sheets to specify the format of the images.

Linking from an image

We have seen how to make a link to another page from text, and you can do the same thing using an image, so that clicking on that image moves you to another page.

The method of doing this is to place the *img* element within the *a* element, that is between the *<a>* and *</a>* opening and closing tags. The *href* attribute of the *<a>* tag gives the address of the link, for example:

```
<a href="boatdetails.html"><img src = "boat.gif" alt = "Sailing boat" height="200" width="180" /></a>
```

This displays an image called *boat.gif.* When it is clicked on, it links to a page in the same folder called *boatdetails.html.* This is shown in Figure 7.2.

Figure 7.2 Using images as links.

When the cursor moves over the image the text specified in the *alt* attribute *sailing boat* is displayed. If the image cannot be found, or if the browser used supports text only, this text is displayed instead of the image.

Image maps

Sometimes you may want different parts of the image to link to different places. You can do this using an image map. These are time consuming to create especially if you want more than a few links.

The first stage in creating an image is to decide how you are going to partition the image so that the parts of it connect to different documents, for example in the image shown in Figure 7.3, four regions have been identified – each corresponds to a different food item, to find out more about that item click on the image.

Figure 7.3 Creating regions for an image map.

The areas chosen for the link do not correspond exactly to the area occupied by the item – since you are limited to three types of area: rectangles, circles and polygons. A polygon is a shape which consists of any number of connected straight lines which form an enclosed shape. The defined areas in Figure 7.3, with the white outline, do not actually appear on the image displayed – they are added here to illustrate the positioning of the areas.

To define these areas, an image editing application which gives you the co-ordinates of points in the image is essential. I usually print the image and mark the co-ordinates on the paper, since it makes it easier to spot mistakes.

The *area* element is used to define these regions. All of these elements must be placed within a *map* element. In this case:

```
<map id = "recipes">
...
</map>
```

The *id* attribute is used to identify this map and to connect it to a particular image in the document.

The map definition is usually placed near the top of the document at the start of the *<body>* section.

Defining Rectangles

On the image shown in Figure 7.3, we need to define a rectangle which contains the *Home* text in the bottom left corner. Open the image in an application such as Paint Shop Pro and note down the co-ordinates of the top left corner and the bottom right corner of the rectangle.

The *area* element for this rectangle is:

```
<area shape = "rect" coords="0,800,150,872" href="home.html" alt = "Home" />
```

- The *shape* attribute states that this shape is a rectangle.
- The *coords* attribute gives the co-ordinates of the top left and bottom right corners.
- The *href* attribute gives the address of the link, in this case to a document in the same folder.
- The *alt* attribute gives the text which is displayed when the cursor moves over the area.

Circles and polygons are defined in a similar way.

Defining Circles

When defining a circle the co-ordinates of the centre of the circle and the radius of the circle are given. The *area* element for the large rectangle containing the tortilla in Figure 7.3 is:

```
<area shape = "circle" coords="360,580,180" href="tortilla.html" alt = "Tortilla" />
```

The *area* element for the area which displays the salad is very similar:

```
<area shape = "circle" coords="448,290,70" href="salad.html" alt = "Salad" />
```

Defining Polygons

The definition of the polygon which contains the image of the bread is a little longer, the *coords* attributes give the position of all the corners which bound the region. These should be given in the sequence in which they occur in the shape, it does not matter if you move around in a clockwise or counter-clockwise direction. The *area* element for this region is shown below:

```
<area shape ="poly" coords="110,0,400,0,0,400,200,370" href="bread.html"
alt ="Bread" />
```

Defining the default region

If you assign a value of *default* for the *shape* attribute you can specify a link if the viewer clicks outside of the defined areas. If you do not want any action to be taken when this occurs you can specify this explicitly with the *nohref* attribute:

```
<area shape = "default" nohref = "nohref" alt = "Food"/>
```

Activating the map

The final stage is to connect the map to an image, this is done by adding the *usemap* attribute to the *img* element which displays the image. This element for the map we have defined is shown below:

```
<img src = "food.png" width="698" height="872" alt = "Food" usemap = "#recipes" /
```

The name of the usemap corresponds to the name given in the *id* attribute in the map definition. Note that a # has been placed in front of the name since it occurs locally in the same document. If it occurred elsewhere you could give a full URL.

The complete body of the XHTML document which defines the map and displays the image is shown below:

```
<body>
<p>
<map id = "recipes">
<area shape = "circle" coords="360,580,180" href="tortilla.html" alt = "Tortilla" />
<area shape = "circle" coords="448,290,70" href="salad.html" alt = "Salad" />
<area shape = "poly" coords="110,0,400,0,0,400,200,370" href="bread.html"
alt = "Bread" />
<area shape = "rect" coords="0,800,150,872" href="home.html" alt = "Home" />
<area shape = "default" nohref = "nohref" alt = "Food"/>
</map>
<img src = "food.png" width="698" height="872" alt = "Food" usemap = "#recipes" />
</p>
</body>
```

If the areas you create partially overlap, it is the earlier definition which is used.

Client and Server side maps

The image maps we have been looking at are called client-side image maps, because they exist within the XHTML document which is downloaded and all the processing takes place locally. It is possible to create server-side maps where the processing takes place on the server. This takes a lot longer, and network traffic is increased since when you click on an area the co-ordinates are sent to the server which sends back an appropriate URL. For these reasons client side mapping is preferred to server side mapping.

Chapter
8

Cascading
Style Sheets

Introduction

When designing a Web site it is important that the same look is maintained throughout the entire site, in terms of the font size and colours and other aspects such as the positioning and borders of images and text. Style sheets, formerly called Cascading Style Sheets (CSS), allow you to define a series of styles and apply them to your web pages. For example you may decide that all text displayed in an *h1* element should be 20pt bold Times Roman. You can specify this in a style sheet, so that wherever this element occurs the formatting is automatically applied. If you decide that the text should be smaller, you simply change the definition in the style sheet and all of the text is automatically reformatted to the new style.

This approach has been used for many years in word processors and desktop publishing applications and is an effective way of ensuring a consistent appearance.

You can achieve the same formatting by using a variety of attributes associated with many elements, but in addition to the problems of maintaining consistency these attributes have been deprecated in XHTML, that is they are supported at the moment, but may not be supported in future releases: in effect if an attribute is deprecated you are being given notice not to use it in future.

The CSS2 specification has been released by the W3C. Fortunately it is fully compatible with CSS1, but adds some extra functionality. The full CSS1 and CSS2 specifications are available from the W3C web site, but they are quite long. The CSS2 specification alone runs to 338 pages, but the key ideas are presented in this chapter.

There is a CSS validator on the W3C web site to which you should submit your style sheets to check their conformance to the XHTML specification.

Types of style sheets

Cascading Style Sheets (CSS), sometimes called just style sheets, contain a set of definitions of the properties of styles used in a document. There are three ways to use style sheets:

- You can place the style sheet within an XHTML document, so that it only applies to that document.
- It can be placed within a separate file, so that it can be used by one or more XHTML documents.
- It can be placed in line - to provide formatting of a specific section of a document.

The preferred technique is to place the style sheet in a separate file, so that you can link to it from every XHTML document in your Web site. However if this is the first time you have used style sheets it is helpful to begin by embedding the style sheet within a document, since it is easier to change it if you make mistakes.

Embedding a style sheet

The first application we are going to look at uses an embedded style sheet to specify the colour and background of text associated with an *h1* and *p* element.

The first stage is to create a simple HTML document which conforms to the Strict DTD specification:

```
<?xml version="1.0" encoding="ISO-8859-1"?>
<!DOCTYPE html PUBLIC "-//W3C//DTD XHTML 1.0 Strict//EN"
"http://www.w3.org/TR/xhtml1/DTD/xhtml1-strict.dtd">
<html xmlns="http://www.w3.org/1999/xhtml">
<head>
<title>Internal style sheet</title>
</head>
<body>
<h1>This is a centred level 1 header in green with a yellow background</h1>
<p>
This paragraph type is red, 14 point sans-serif font with the default background
```

```
colour</p>
</body>
</html>
```

At the moment the document uses the default colours and alignment.

The embedded style sheet is placed immediately after the closing *</title>* tag and has this format:

```
<style type = "text/css">
<!--
-->
</style>
```

- The *<style>* tag states that this is the beginning of a style sheet definition.
- The *type* attribute indicates the type of the style sheet specification used.
- The *<!--   -->* pair indicate that everything placed between them will be regarded as a comment (and therefore no action taken) by browsers which do not support style sheets.
- The *</style>* tag ends the element.

The style sheet codes are placed within the comment pair.

Style sheet codes

The style sheet codes have the following format:

```
selector {property : value; property : value}
```

- The *selector* is the name of what we are controlling the format of, for example the *h1* element.
- The *property* is the property that we are specifying, for example, the colour or font size.
- The *value* is the value assigned to the property, for example, red to a colour property.

You can have as many property/value pairs as necessary: note that they are separated by a semi-colon character.

For example, to change the characteristics of *p* elements so that all text is red, sans-serif with a 14pt font size:

```
p {
color: red;
font-size:14pt;
font-family: sans-serif
}
```

To change the style of the *h1* element so that its text is green on a yellow background, and is aligned in the centre of the screen:

```
h1 {
color :green;
background : yellow;
text-align: center
}
```

The entire document is given below:

```
<?xml version="1.0" encoding="ISO-8859-1"?>
<!DOCTYPE html PUBLIC "-//W3C//DTD XHTML 1.0 Strict//EN"
"http://www.w3.org/TR/xhtml1/DTD/xhtml1-strict.dtd">
<html xmlns="http://www.w3.org/1999/xhtml">
<head>
<title>Internal style sheet</title>
<style type="text/css">
<!--
p {
color: red;
font-size:14pt;
font-family: sans-serif
}
h1 {
color :green;
background : yellow;
text-align: center
}
-->
</style>
</head>
<body>
<h1>This is a centred level 1 header in green with a yellow background</h1>
```

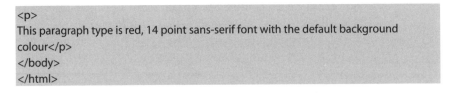

```
<p>
This paragraph type is red, 14 point sans-serif font with the default background
colour</p>
</body>
</html>
```

This document is shown in Figure 8.1.

Figure 8.1 *Using an internal style sheet.*

The background colour used for the *p* element is the default, however it is good practice to explicitly state what the background is. If you do not, your document may not appear exactly as you intended. If you fail to give the background, the CSS validator on the W3C web site will give a warning.

We are going to look at how to specify the style sheet codes in more detail, but first let's see how the same effect can be produced using a style sheet in a separate file.

Linking to a style sheet

The external style sheet contains exactly the same information as the embedded style sheet, apart from explicitly specifying the background colour of the *p* element rather than relying on the default. This is not mandatory, but avoids a warning when the CSS is validated:

```css
p {
color: red;
background : white;
font-size:14pt;
font-family: sans-serif
}
h1 {
color :green;
background : yellow;
text-align: center
}
```

This has been placed in a file called mystyle.css.

To link to this style sheet, the *link* element is placed below the title element in place of the embedded style sheet:

```html
<link rel="stylesheet" href="mystyle.css" type="text/css" />
```

This connects to the style sheet called *mystyle.css* in the same folder.

The new XHTML file is shown below:

```html
<?xml version="1.0" encoding="ISO-8859-1"?>
<!DOCTYPE html PUBLIC "-//W3C//DTD XHTML 1.0 Strict//EN"
"http://www.w3.org/TR/xhtml1/DTD/xhtml1-strict.dtd">
<html xmlns="http://www.w3.org/1999/xhtml">
<head>
<title>External style sheet</title>
<link rel="stylesheet" href="mystyle.css" type="text/css" />
</head>
<body>
<h1>This is a centred level 1 header in green with a yellow background
</h1>
<p>
This paragraph type is red, 14 point sans-serif font with the default background colour
</p>
</body>
</html>
```

The advantage of using this approach is that we can place a link to the style sheet from as many documents as we wish - this makes it easy to maintain a consistent look to your web site and can be used to ensure that all web pages conform to a company standard. If you want to change the style throughout all your documents you only have to change the one style sheet document.

Applying styles to more than one element

If you want to apply styles to all of the basic elements in a set of documents, you can place formatting information in between the opening and closing body elements in the style sheet, for example:

```
body {
color : blue;
background : white;
margin-left:50pt;
font-style: italic;
font-size : 20pt;
font-family: courier
}
```

If you only want to set the characteristics of a few elements, you can list them before the formatting information, for example:

```
h1, h2, h3 {
    color : green;
    background : yellow;
    text-align : center
    }
```

The formatting will apply to *h1*, *h2* and *h3* elements.

In-line formatting

You can use in-line styles which apply to a specific part of a document, but this is counter to the philosophy of XHTML which encourages the use of style sheets (especially in a separate file) rather than embedding the formatting of individual elements in the XHTML document. Nevertheless it is still sometimes useful, when an existing style has a complex set of properties and on one occasion you wish to modify it slightly, perhaps changing the text to a different colour for emphasis.

To apply in-line colours the *style* attribute is added to the element as shown below:

```
<h1 style = "color : green; background : yellow; text-align : center">
This is a centred level 1 header in green with a yellow background</h1>
<p style = "color : red; font-size : 14; font-family : sans-serif">
This paragraph type is red, 14 point sans-serif font with the default background colour
</p>
```

This achieves the same formatting as the previous examples, however any following headers and paragraphs will not use this formatting: they will use the default format. Note the semicolons which separate the style components.

Classes and IDs

Classes and IDs are a way of modifying an element's style, if for example you want to create a paragraph of text which has all the same characteristics as other paragraphs (as defined in the style sheet) but has a larger font, you can do this by creating a class or ID. The difference between classes and IDs is that an ID can only be used once, while a class can be applied many times. In practice, most browsers allow you to apply an ID more than once, however this is contrary to the Strict XHTML specification.

Creating and using IDs

An ID consists of two parts:

- A # character and a name. The name should reflect what it is that the ID does.
- A set of characteristics enclosed in a { } pair, for example.

To see how this works in practice we are going to define a style and modify it using two IDs.

The style for the *h1* element is:

```
h1 {
color: red;
background : white;
font-size:18pt;
text-align: left;
font-family: sans-serif;
}
```

If we want to preserve these characteristics, but make the font size small and italic, we can define an ID:

```
#small {font-size: 12pt; font-style:italic}
```

To define another ID which is larger and oblique:

```
#large {font-size: 24pt; font-style:oblique }
```

To use the IDs you must specify the name of the ID in the *id* attribute, for example:

```
<h1>Why chocolate is good for you(18pt)</h1>
<h1 id = "small">Frequently asked questions(12pt italic)</h1>
<h1 id = "large">Nutritional value(24pt oblique)</h1>
```

This produces the document shown in Figure 8.2.

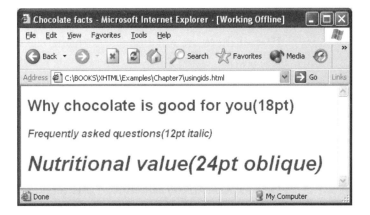

Figure 8.2 Using IDs.

You can ensure that an ID may be applied only to a particular element type, by preceding the # with the name of that element for example:

```
p#small {font-size : 12pt; font-style : italic}
```

This only allows the ID to be applied only to a *p* element.

If you wish to modify a style in the same way more than once you should define and use a class.

Creating and using classes

The syntactic differences between defining and using an ID and a class are small: in place of a # a period character is used, for example:

```
.small {font-size: 12pt; font-style:italic}
.large {font-size: 24pt; font-style:oblique}
```

When using the class, instead of using the *id* attribute, the *class* attribute used:

```
<h1>Why chocolate is good for you(18pt)</h1>
<h1 class = "small">Frequently asked questions(12pt italic)</h1>
<h1 class = "large">Nutritional value(24pt oblique)</h1>
```

Since it is no more complicated to use a class rather than an ID and there are advantages to using classes it is best to use classes rather than IDs as there is a possibility that in the future you may wish to use the characteristics defined in an ID more than once.

Creating a style sheet

We have seen how to create a basic style sheet and to link it with an XHTML document. In this section we are going to look at the features which you can specify in a style sheet. These features are:

- Font properties.
- Text properties.
- Colour.
- Creating boxes.
- Positioning properties.
- Media types.

Font properties

One of the difficulties of designing XHTML documents is that you may not be sure of the capabilities of the computer which will be used to view the document. This is a common problem when specifying the font which is to be used, since you do not know what fonts are available on the target machine.

There are two possible ways of minimizing this problem, you can either specify a list of fonts: if the first is not available, the second is used and so on. If none are available the default font is used, for example:

```
p {
background : white;
font-family: arial, times
}
```

The background colour is specified to avoid a warning when using the W3C validator.

If the font name has a space, such as courier new, the name should be included in quotes:

```
h1 {
background : white;
font-family : "courier new", "courier narrow", myriad
}
```

The other alternative is to specify a font family rather than a specific font. Font families define a set of characteristics which a font must have. There are five font families available:

Table 8.1 Font families.

Font family	Typical members
serif	Times, Palatino.
sans-serif	Helvetica, Arial.
cursive	Zapf Chancery.
fantasy	Western, Circus.
monospace	Courier, System.

For example:

```
h2 {
background : white;
font-family : monospace
}
```

The problem with using font families is that the font which is used is different depending on both the browser and the operating system. For example, if you specify a font family of monospace, this corresponds to Courier New on a PC and Monaco on a Mac. The fantasy font family corresponds to Ariel bold on a PC using Netscape 6, Brush Script MS on a PC using Internet Explorer 6 and Times on a Mac using Internet Explorer.

The only way in which you can be sure that your documents will display as you wish is to view them on a wide variety of platforms with a variety of browsers. A defensive way of specifying your font would be to list similar fonts for different platforms and finally a font family which will be used if none of the specific fonts you list are found, as shown below:

```
h3 {
background : white;
font-family : courier, monaco, monospace
}
```

This may not be ideal, but it is probably better than relying on the default.

Font characteristics

There are four characteristics of fonts which you can control in addition to the *font-family*, these are shown in Table 8.2.

Table 8.2 Controlling font characteristics.

Property	Values
font-size	xx-small | x-small | small | medium | large | x-large | xx-large | smaller | larger | a numerical value followed by a valid unit | n%.
font-style	normal | italic | oblique.
font-variant	normal | small-caps.
font-weight	bold | extra-bold | bolder | lighter | 100 | 200 | 300 | 400 | 500 | 600 | 700 | 800| 900.

In Table 8.2, when you specify a numerical value (unless it is a percentage), you must follow it with a valid unit: for example:

```
p {
font-size: 10mm;
}
```

There are a wide variety of units which follow the numerical size:

- *in*, *mm* and *cm* are the most obvious, they are short for: inch, millimetre and centimetre.

- *pc* and *pt* are short for pica and point. A pica is 1/6 of an inch and a point is 1/72 of an inch.
- *px* stands for pixel.
- *em* and *ex* are different from the others in that they specify a relative size. An *em* is equal to the current font size, so for example, if the current font size is 12pt, 2em is 24 pt. Strictly speaking in typographic terms it is the width of the character 'M' in the current font. An *ex* is the height of the character 'x' in the current font.

The meanings of the other font properties are clear from their names.

You can use as many of the font characteristics as you wish, but it is advisable that you keep to the order given below, some browsers do not interpret them correctly if the order is different.

- *font-style*, *font-weight* and *font-variant* should come first. It does not matter in which order they appear.
- *font-size*.
- *font-family*.

for example:

```
p {
background : white;
font-style: italic;
font-weight: bold;
font-size: 10mm;
font-family: times, sans-serif;
}
```

There is a quick way of specifying these attributes:

```
p {
background : white;
font : italic bold 10mm times, sans-serif;
}
```

This is functionally exactly the same.

Text properties

In addition to controlling all the characteristics of fonts you can specify some features of text. These text properties are listed in Table 8.3.

When a numeric value may be specified as in the case of the last four items in Table 8.2, the units used must always be given.

Table 8.3 Text properties.

Property	Values
text-align	*center* | *left* | *right* | *justify*.
text-decoration	*none* | *underline* | *overline* | *line-through* | *blink*.
text-transform	*none* | *capitalize* | *uppercase* | *lowercase*.
vertical-align	*baseline* | *super* | *sub* | *top* | *middle* | *bottom* | *text-top* | *text-bottom* | n%.
letter-spacing	A numerical value followed by a valid unit.
word-spacing	A numerical value followed by a valid unit.
text-indent	A numerical value followed by a valid unit | n%.
line-height	A numerical value followed by a valid unit | n%.

One unexpected feature of the *text-indent* property is that it only applies to the first line as shown in Figure 8.3.

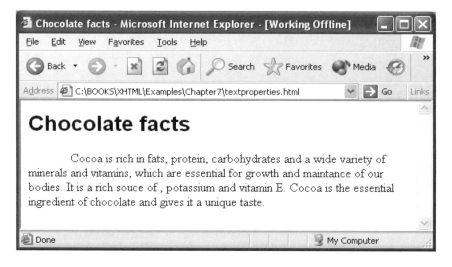

Figure 8.3 Indenting text.

The style sheet used to create Figure 8.3 has a *text-indent* property of 40pt:

```
p {
font-size : 12pt;
text-align: left;
text-decoration: none;
text-indent: 40pt;
font-family: times;
}
h1 {
font: bold 30pt arial, sans-serif;
}
```

If you want to indent the whole paragraph, you must use the *margin* property which we are going to look at next.

The margin property

Controlling document margins in HTML has always been difficult. Since it was not possible to do it directly, Web designers had to resort to using blank image files or empty tables to create the impression that there was more white space around a document. This is no longer necessary. There are four margin properties: *margin-left*, *margin-right*, *margin-top*, *margin-bottom*, for example:

```
body {
        margin-top : 40pt;
        margin-left : 20pt;
        margin-right : 30pt;
        margin-bottom : 50pt;
        }
```

You do not need to specify all of the margins, just the ones you require. A quick way of writing these four properties is to combine them into a single statement

```
body { margin : 40pt 20pt 30pt 50pt }
```

You must specify all four values in the order, *top*, *left*, *right* and *bottom*.

Colour properties

XHTML recognizes the red, green, blue (rgb) colour model. Combining these colours can create any colour. There are five ways in which you can specify colours, for example the following all represent blue:

- *color : blue.* There are sixteen standard colours which can be specified by name.
- *color : #0000ff.* Each of the two pairs of hexadecimal digits represents the amount of red, green and blue in the colour. The minimum value for each pair is 00, the largest is ff.
- *color : #00f.* Each of the digits is duplicated (in this case to 0000ff) to specify the rgb components.
- *color : rgb(0%, 0%, 100%).* Each of the components is given as a percentage between 0 and 100.
- *color : rgb(0,0,255).* Each of the components is given as a value between 0 and 255.

You can use any of these methods, but it is good to choose one style and stick with it.

The following code defines a *p* element as red, 18pt sans-serif text.

```
p {
    color : red;
    font-size : 18pt;
    font-family : sans-serif;
}
```

Box properties

A useful feature of XHTML is that you can put boxes around paragraphs usually for emphasis. Some essential properties of boxes are shown in Table 8.4:

Table 8.4 Box properties.

Property	Values
border-color	A valid colour.
border-style	*none*| *dotted*| *dashed*| *solid*| *double*| *groove*| *ridge*| *inset*| *outset*.
border-width	A numerical value and a valid unit | *thick*| *medium*| *thin*.
float	*left*| *right*| *none*.
height	A numerical measurement and a valid unit | *auto*.
width	A numerical measurement and a valid unit | *auto*.
margin-bottom	A numerical measurement and a valid unit | n%.
margin-top	A numerical measurement and a valid unit | n%.
margin-left	A numerical measurement and a valid unit | n%.
margin-right	A numerical measurement and a valid unit | n%.

The *float* properties determines where a box is placed in relation to the text.

The code below shows a style sheet called boxes.css which uses a few of these properties in the style for *h2* elements.

```
h1 {
color:red;
background : white;
font-size:18pt;
text-align: left;
font-family: sans-serif;
 }
p {
color: black;
background : white;
font-size:10pt;
font-family: sans-serif;
 }
h2 {
color: red;
background : white;
font-size:16pt;
width:40%;
border-color : black;
border-style : solid;
border-width : 1mm;
float: right
}
```

The head and body of a document attached to this style sheet is shown below. The page displayed in Figure 8.4 is produced.

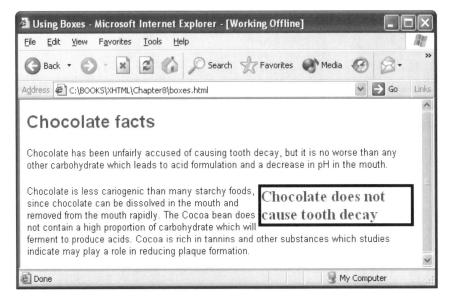

Figure 8.4 Boxing paragraphs.

```
<head>
<title>Using Boxes</title>
<link rel="stylesheet" href = "boxes.css" type="text/css" />
</head>
<body>
<h1>Chocolate facts</h1>
<p>
Chocolate has been unfairly accused of causing tooth decay, but it is no worse than any
other carbohydrate which leads to acid formulation and a decrease in pH in the mouth.
</p>
<h2>
Chocolate does not cause tooth decay
</h2>
<p>
Chocolate is less cariogenic than many starchy foods, since chocolate can be dissolved
in the mouth and removed from the mouth rapidly. The Cocoa bean does not contain a
high proportion of carbohydrate which will ferment to produce acids.  Cocoa is rich in
tannins and other substances which studies indicate may play a role in reducing
```

```
plaque formation.
</p>
</body>
```

If you wish, you can combine the *border*, *color*, *style* and *width* properties into a single property for example:

```
border : black solid 1mm;
```

produces exactly the same effect as:

```
border-color : black;
border-style : solid;
border-width : 1mm;
```

Note that in the shorthand form, all three values must be supplied and they must be in the order: *color*, *style*, and *width*.

Changing anchor colours

It is important that links are clearly visible on the page - the convention is to underline the link and give it a different colour. There are four possible states which a link may have:

- Normal. A link has not been clicked and the mouse is not over it.
- Visited. A link has recently been clicked. The amount of time which the link will stay this colour is configurable in the browser.
- Selected. A link is in the process of being clicked, that is the mouse has been pressed, but not released.
- Hover. The mouse is over the link.

You can change the colour of the links in these states:

```
a{color : red}
a : selected{color : green}
a : visited {color : blue}
a : hover {color : orange}
```

Positioning attributes

If you wish you can specify the exact position of text and images on the page.

It can be useful to position a few images in a specific position on a page, however if it is used for more than this, it can cause problems. It is very time consuming working out the co-ordinates of where items should be placed and since you do not know the capabilities of the computer which will be used to view the document the results may not be what you wanted.

There are five positioning properties, shown in Table 8.5.

Table 8.5 Positioning properties.

Property	Values
position	*static* | *relative* | *absolute* | *inherit.*
top	A numerical value followed by a valid unit | n% | *auto* | *inherit.*
bottom	A numerical value followed by a valid unit | n% | *auto* | *inherit.*
right	A numerical value followed by a valid unit | n% | *auto* | *inherit.*
left	A numerical value followed by a valid unit | n% | *auto* | *inherit.*

The *position* property has four possible values:

- *static.* Positions the item in the normal in-line position.
- *relative.* Positions the item in-line, but with a position which is adjusted relative to the normal flow of the document.
- *absolute.* Positions the item in an absolute position irrespective of all other items.
- *inherit.* The same positioning as the parent element.

The *top*, *bottom*, *right* and *left* properties may all be set to the same values:

- A numerical value followed by a valid unit.
- n%. A percentage of the available space.
- *auto.* The default value based on the content.
- *inherit.* The same as the parent element.

A typical example of where you might want to specify the absolute of an item is shown in Figure 8.5.

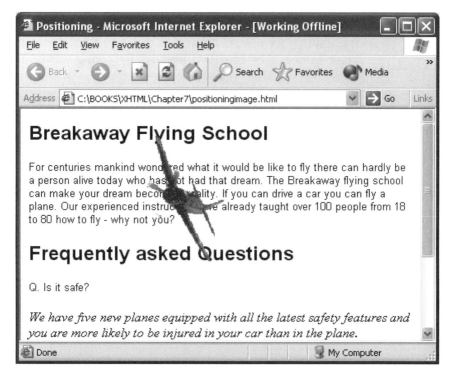

Figure 8.5 Positioning images.

You could specify the position using ID or classes, but since the position of each item will be different it is one of the few occasions where it is easier to use in-line styles.

The two text paragraphs are specified in the standard way - without any positioning being given. The aeroplane image is a GIF file with a transparent background.

The display and positioning is controlled as shown below:

```
<img src="transparent.gif" alt ="Aeroplane" height="200" width="180"
style = "position: absolute; left:100; top:10" />
```

The position of the image has no impact on the text - it is positioned as if the image does not exist.

If you want to ensure that there is no overlap, you may have to use positioning for all the items on the page, for example to achieve the page shown in Figure 8.6.

Specifying absolute positions can cause problems, but to some extend they can be alleviated by giving widths in percentages rather than absolute numbers. This will ensure that the relative size of items remains the same.

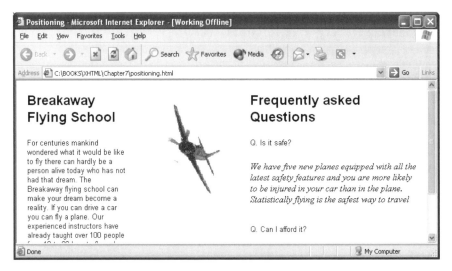

Figure 8.6 Absolute positioning.

The head and body of this document is shown below, the *style* attribute is applied to every element:

```
<head>
<title>Positioning</title>
<link rel="stylesheet" href ="positioning.css" type="text/css" />
</head>
<body>
<h1 style = "position : absolute; left : 20; top = 20; width = 180">
Breakaway Flying School
</h1>
<p style = "position : absolute; left : 20; top = 100; width = 180">
For centuries mankind wondered what it would be like to fly.  There can hardly be a
person alive today who has not had that dream.  The Breakaway flying school can make
your dream become a reality.  If you can drive a car you can fly a plane.  Our
```

```
experienced instructors have already taught over 100 people from 18 to 80 how to fly -
why not you?
</p>
<p>
<img src="transparent.gif" alt ="Aeroplane" height="200" width="180"
style ="position: absolute; left:220; top:20" />
</p>
<h1 style = "position : absolute; left : 420; top = 20; width = 300">
Frequently asked Questions </h1>
<p style = "position : absolute; left : 420; top = 100; width = 300">
Q. Is it safe?
</p>
<address style = "position : absolute; left : 420; top = 140; width = 300">
We have five new planes equipped with all the latest safety features and you are more
likely to be injured in your car than in the plane.  Statistically flying is the safest way to
travel
</address>
<p style = "position : absolute; left : 420; top = 250; width = 300">
Q. Can I afford it?
</p>
<address style = "position : absolute; left : 420; top = 290; width = 300">
We have an new lost cost program so that you can start to fly with just a single
payment of $50.  We have a variety of different easy pay schemes designed to fit all
pockets.  Call us now for a quote.
</address>
</body>
```

All of the items on the left of the image start 20 pixels from the left of the window and have a width of 180 pixels.

All of the items on the right of the image have a *left* position of 420 and a width of 300.

The *top* position determines how far down the column the element appears.

Using layers

Style sheets support layering, that is you can specify the order in which text and images are placed on the page by giving them a z-order.

The higher the z-number, the nearer the item is to the front of the display.

Figure 8.7 Using z-order.

Figure 8.7 shows the text *Chocolate News* with a shadow effect. Each of the lines is in fact the text written twice, the dark text is black, the lighter text is cyan. The top and left position of black text is slightly reduced.

The only difference between the first line of text displayed and the second is that in the first line the z-index of the cyan text is 1 and that of the black text 2. Therefore the black text appears to be on top. The z-index of the second line of text is reversed so that the cyan text appears on top:

```
<head>
<title>Z-order</title>
<link rel="stylesheet" href ="zorder.css" type="text/css" />
 </head>
<body>
<h1 style="font-size:50; position:absolute; left:10; top=20; z-index=2">
Chocolate News
</h1>
<h1 style="font-size:50; color:cyan; position:absolute; left:14; top=24; z-index=1">
Chocolate News
</h1>
```

```
<h1 style="font-size:50; position:absolute; left:10; top=80; z-index=1">
Chocolate News
</h1>
<h1 style="font-size:50; color:cyan; position:absolute; left:14; top=84; z-index=2">
Chocolate News
</h1>
</body>
```

Media types properties

An interesting and useful aspect of the second version of style sheets (CSS2) is that you may incorporate instructions within the style sheet which will display in a different way depending on the media type, for example, the requirements for a computer with a large monitor are very different from those of a hand-held (PDA) type device.

You can use the @media rule to specify different characteristics for different media types.

The media types supported are:

- aural. Speech synthesizers.
- braille. Tactile braile equipment.
- embossed. Paged braille printers.
- handheld. Small screen PDA type devices.
- print. Paged, printed material or for print preview on screen.
- projection. Projected presentations or transparancies.
- screen. Colour computer screens.
- tty. Fixed pitch devices such as teletypes.
- tv. Television type devices, typically colour, low resolution.

You can include multiple instructions within the style sheet, for example:

```
@media print {
      body { font-size : 12pt}
}
@media handheld {
      body { font-size : 9pt}
```

```
}
@media screen. print, projection {
     body { font-family: Arial}
}
```

In place of one or more of the media types you could use *all*.

Unfortunately this facility is not currently supported by any popular browser.

Changing the background

There are three properties which may be used for controlling the background of your document as shown in Table 8.6. The properties should be defined in the document style sheet.

Table 8.6 Background properties.

Property	Values
background-color	A valid colour.
background-image	url(a valid URL) | none.
background-repeat	repeat | repeat-x | repeat-y | none.

The *background-color* property is the most straightforward to use, for example:

```
body{
     background-color : cyan
}
```

You can also specify a background image using the *background-image* property. If the image is not sufficient to completely fill the document, you can have the image repeated using the *background-repeat* property:

```
body{
background-image: url(background.png);
background-repeat: repeat;
}
```

If the *background-repeat* property is assigned to *repeat*, the background is tiled as shown in Figure 8.8. This the default if no value is assigned to this property.

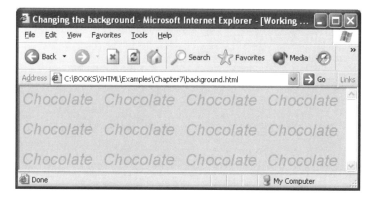

Figure 8.8 changing the background.

You may also specify that the picture should repeat only in either a horizontal or vertical fashion.

Conflicting properties

Have you wondered why style sheets are sometimes called Cascading Style Sheets? It is because of the way in which conflicts in the value of a property are resolved. For example, some text may be defined as red in one place and green in another. Which takes precedence? There are two simple rules, which we have already used implicitly:

- The latest instruction is used in preference to a previous one.
- If there is a conflict between a more general property value, for example, a text size defined in the body of a style sheet and one defined for a particular element, such as *h1*. The definition which is most specific will override the other. In this case, the property as defined especially for *h1* will be used, even if it occurs after the other definition.

Chapter 9

Creating and Using Frames

Introduction

Frames allow you to break down the viewing area of the browser in to a number of regions, each region showing a different Web page. This has a number of advantages, if, for example, you have a header, or a list of links on more than one page, the header and links could be placed in frames and only downloaded once, however many pages are viewed on the site. It is also easier to update the header and links pages since the same documents are viewed on every page.

Frames have gained a reputation for being difficult to use and for producing unattractive, problematic sites. The border between the frames takes up space and if a lower resolution than 800×600 is used, a site with frames can quickly seem too crowded. If the whole of a frame does not fit into the space available, horizontal and vertical scrollbars may be added taking up even more space and making the site even less attractive. There were also some technical problems with earlier browsers which meant that the back button did not work correctly. Some browsers did not support frames fully and therefore you needed to create an alternative site without frames.

In the past few years, most users have moved to higher resolution screens and the technical problems with the earlier browsers have been overcome. You may have to provide an alternative set of pages which do not use frames, but the latest browsers are available free or at very low cost, so most users are no longer using old browsers which do not support frames, and it may be sufficient to simply display a courtesy message saying that the site requires an up-to-date browser.

You can duplicate many of the features of frames with tables, but a site with frames will download faster and with careful design can be used to create an attractive and efficient Web site.

Types of frames

XHTML supports two type of frames:

- Fixed frames divide the screen into different parts, each part contains a separate document. Clicking on a link usually only changes one of the documents which are displayed.
- In-line frames are used to display a document entirely within another document.

We are going to look at each of these types.

Creating fixed frames

If you want to create fixed frames, you must first create a frameset document which specifies where the other documents are to be displayed. The frameset document does not contain any other information.

The first stage is to create the frameset document. To do this you must use the Frameset DTD rather than the Strict or Transitional DTD which we have been using so far. Your XHTML document should start by specifying this:

```
<!DOCTYPE html PUBLIC "-//W3C//DTD XHTML 1.0 Frameset//EN"
"http://www.w3.org/TR/xhtml1/DTD/xhtml1-frameset.dtd">
<html xmlns = "http://www.w3.org/1999/xhtml">
```

The next stage is to create the documents which are to be displayed within the frame. In this case we are going to display the document shown in Figure 9.1.

These two documents are virtually empty, so we can focus on the frameset document.

The two documents displayed are called left.html and right.html. The opening *<frameset>* tag is used to specify the size of the two pages:

```
<frameset cols="50%, 50%">
```

In this case each of the pages takes up 50% of the available width.

Figure 9.1 Using a frame with two columns.

The two columns are first given a name and the XHTML document which is displayed in each column is given next:

```
<frame name="left" src="left.html" />
<frame name="right" src="right.html" />
```

The first column is called *left* (we use this name to refer to it within the XHTML) and displays an XHTML document called *left.html*. Similarly the right column is called *right* and contains a file called *right.html*. There is no relationship between the name of the region and the name of the document, however it can make it easier to understand what is going on if you give the region the same name as the file.

The *frameset* element is ended with its closing tag:

```
</frameset>
```

The page shown in Figure 9.1 is displayed. The entire frameset file is shown below:

```
<?xml version="1.0" encoding="ISO-8859-1"?>
<!DOCTYPE html PUBLIC "-//W3C//DTD XHTML 1.0 Frameset//EN"
"http://www.w3.org/TR/xhtml1/DTD/xhtml1-frameset.dtd">
<html xmlns="http://www.w3.org/1999/xhtml">
```

```
<head>
<title>Using vertical frames</title>
<link href = "style.css" type="text/css" rel="stylesheet" />
</head>
<frameset cols="50%, 50%">
<frame name="left" src="left.html" />
<frame name="right" src="right.html" />
</frameset>
</html>
```

You can create horizontal frames in a similar way as shown in Figure 9.2:

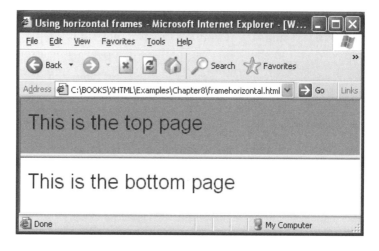

Figure 9.2 *Using a frame with two rows.*

The only difference is that instead of using the *cols* attribute in the frameset element, you use the *rows* attribute to give what proportion of the vertical space is allocated to each of the documents:

```
<frameset rows="50%, 50%">
<frame name="top" src="top.html" />
<frame name="bottom" src="bottom.html" />
</frameset>
```

The two documents displayed are called top.html and bottom.html and their positions reflect this.

Before we look at how to create more complex framesets and how to control the appearance of frames we are going to look in more detail at how to specify the size of each of the frames.

Controlling frame size

The size of the frames is crucial to the appearance of your site, unfortunately it can be difficult to decide since you do not usually know the resolution of the screen which will be used to view the site. In addition, the browser and the operating system both have an impact on how the site will appear. If you are creating a serious site, you always need to check how your site will appear using a range of popular configurations. This is particularly important when using frames where the impact of different set-ups is much greater.

These considerations have a bearing on how you specify the size of the frames. There are a variety of options:

- You can give the sizes as a percentage, for example:

<frameset cols = "50%, 50%">

The percentages should add up to 100, however if they do not, most browsers seem to treat the percentages as relative measurements, that is if you specify two columns , one 40% and the other 10%, the first column will be four times as wide as the second column.

- You can use pixels, for example:

<frameset cols = "300, 100">

however, it is unlikely that the total width you give in pixels will be same as the width of the viewing screen. Most browsers use the pixel sizes as relative measurements, for example, a frame given as 300 pixels will be three times the width as one given as 100 pixels.

- You can use an asterisk. This is usually used to indicate that all the remaining space should be used, for example:

```
<frameset cols = "300, *">
```

This will make the left column 300 pixels wide and the second will take up all the remaining space.

- You can use the asterisk to indicate the relative size of rows or columns, for example:

```
<frameset cols = "*, 2*">
```

This means that the second row will be twice as wide as the first row.

- You can even combine the asterisk with the other methods, for example:

```
<frameset cols = "20%, 200, 2*, *">
```

This means that the first column will occupy 20% of the width. The second column 200 pixels. The browser calculates the remaining space and allocates twice as much of that space to the third column as the fourth.

The leftmost column is usually used to display a list of links, so the most widely used approach is to give this column a fixed size in pixels and to use asterisks to specify how the remaining space is to be divided.

This was the approach used in an early version of the Essential series web site (www.essential-series.com) shown in Figure 9.3.

When the size of the browser window is changed, the left column remains the same. This is not a problem if you have a 17in monitor, but if you are using a laptop or a desktop computer with a smaller screen the content frame on the right can seem small.

Figure 9.3   *An early version of the Essential series web site using frames.*

Creating more complex framesets

Many pages use only columns or rows, but some, such as the page shown in Figure 9.4 have a more complex layout, combining rows and columns. The top and left frames are found on every page. The right frame changes and displays the content.

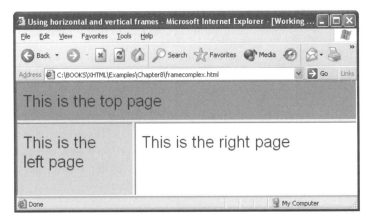

Figure 9.4   *Combining multiple columns and rows.*

```
<frameset rows="40%, *">
```

The name and URL of the document which is displayed in the top row is specified next:

```
<frame name="top" src="top.html" />
```

Rather than giving the name and URL of the second row, another *frameset* element is specified:

```
<frameset cols="200, *">
```

This divides the second row into two columns, which are given next:

```
<frame name="left" src="left.html" />
<frame name="right" src="right.html" />
```

Finally both the frameset elements are closed:

```
</frameset>
</frameset>
```

The complete code is shown below:

```
<?xml version="1.0" encoding="ISO-8859-1"?>
<!DOCTYPE html PUBLIC "-//W3C//DTD XHTML 1.0 Frameset//EN"
"http://www.w3.org/TR/xhtml1/DTD/xhtml1-frameset.dtd">
<html xmlns="http://www.w3.org/1999/xhtml">
<head>
<title>Using horizontal and vertical frames</title>
<link href = "style.css" type="text/css" rel="stylesheet" />
</head>
<frameset rows="40%, *">
<frame name="top" src="top.html" />
<frameset cols="200, *">
<frame name="left" src="left.html" />
<frame name="right" src="right.html" />
</frameset>
</frameset>
</html>
```

This approach can be used to create more complex layouts, for example that shown in Figure 9.5.

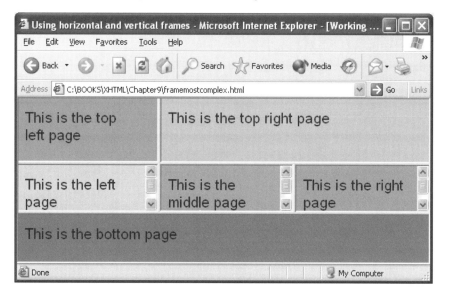

Figure 9.5 *A complex layout.*

The XHTML used to create Figure 9.5 is shown below:

```
<?xml version="1.0" encoding="ISO-8859-1"?>
<!DOCTYPE html PUBLIC "-//W3C//DTD XHTML 1.0 Frameset//EN"
"http://www.w3.org/TR/xhtml1/DTD/xhtml1-frameset.dtd">
<html xmlns="http://www.w3.org/1999/xhtml">
<head>
<title>Using horizontal and vertical frames</title>
<link href = "style.css" type="text/css" rel="stylesheet" />
</head>
<frameset rows="40%, *, *">
<frameset cols="200, *">
<frame name="topleft" src="topleft.html" />
<frame name="topright" src="topright.html" />
</frameset>
<frameset cols="200, *, *">
<frame name="left" src="left.html" />
<frame name="middle" src="middle.html" />
<frame name="right" src="right.html" />
</frameset>
```

```
<frame name="bottom" src="bottom.html" />
</frameset>
</html>
```

- The frameset is initially given three rows, the first 40% of the available space and the second two half the remaining space each.
- The top row is divided into two columns (topleft and topright).
- The second row is divided into three columns, left, middle and right.
- Finally the bottom row contains a single document called bottom.

It can seem difficult to construct these more complex framesets, fortunately they are rarely needed - simple framesets with only a few columns and rows usually produce the most satisfactory pages.

One aspect of poor design which is sometimes seen on Web sites is the use of frames within a frame - this invariably looks awful.

Preventing frame resizing

If you design a document with frames, the borders can be dragged and resized by people viewing the document. If you have spent a long time designing the look of your document you probably want to stop this happening. You can do this by using the *noresize* attribute, for example:

```
<frame name = "left" src = "left.html" noresize = "noresize" />
<frame name = "right" src = "right.html" noresize = "noresize"/>
```

Setting one frame so that it cannot resize also prevents adjacent frames from resizing. Since the two frames above are adjacent, the same effect could be obtained by setting the *noresize* attribute for just one of them. However, it is recommended that you make it explicit which frames you do not want resized.

Formatting

There are three ways in which you can control the appearance of frames:

- Controlling the use of scrollbars.
- Changing the appearance of the frame borders.
- Controlling frame margins.

We are going to look at each of these.

Scrollbars

By default, if the space allocated for a document is not large enough, vertical or horizontal scroll bars are added as required. This can have a major impact on the appearance of your Web site, since the scrollbars themselves take up space, making the situation even worse. You can control the use of scrollbars by using the *scrolling* attribute. This attribute can have one of three values:

- *auto*. This is the default. Scrollbars are added as required.
- *yes*. Both horizontal and vertical scrollbars are displayed whether they are needed or not.
- *no*. No scrollbars are displayed even if they are required.

For example:

```
<frame name = "top" src = "top.html" noresize = "noresize" scrolling = "no"/>
```

This is a problematic attribute, since you do not need to specify the *auto* value - you can just rely on the default. Assigning the value *yes* to the attribute is not likely to be used since it is hard to think of any situation where you would want scrollbars to be added when they are not required. The *no* value for this attribute is the only one which is likely to be used, however this must be used with caution. If you have a frame which contains text which cannot fit entirely into the space provided, perhaps because it is being viewed using a low resolution screen, and you do not allow scrollbars to be added, it will be impossible to see some of the text. If it is clear that some text is missing at least the viewer is aware of a problem. However, if the frame contains a list of links and a few cannot be seen, the viewer will not be aware of this.

Frame borders

The frame border can be controlled by two attributes:

- *frameborder.* Controls the width of the border. A value of 0 removes the border. The default is 1.
- *bordercolor.* Specifes the colour of the border.

The effect of the *frameborder* attribute varies depending on the browser used, in particular there are differences between Internet Explorer and Netscape, and even differences between versions of the same browser, so this attribute should be used with caution.

Figure 9.6 shows how the page displayed in Figure 9.5 changes when the *frameborder* attribute is assigned to 0.

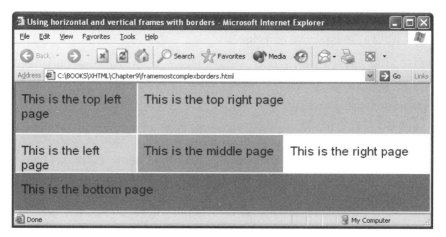

Figure 9.6 Changing borders.

An example of using the *frameborder* attribute is given below:

```
<frame name = "topleft" src = "topleft.html"  frameborder = "0" scrolling = "no" />
```

The *bordercolor* attribute is deprecated and so should be avoided, however it is supported by most browsers. It requires a standard colour in any of the usual formats, for example:

```
<frame name = "topleft" src = "topleft.html" bordercolor = "red"  scrolling = "no" />
```

The appearance does vary depending on the browser used.

Frame margins

You can control the size of the margins with two attributes:

- *marginheight*. Determines the size of both the top and botton margins.
- *marginwidth*. Determines the size of both the left and right margins.

For example:

```
<frame name="topright" src="topright.html"  frameborder="1"
marginheight="100" marginwidth="50"  noresize ="noresize" scrolling="no" />
```

assigns the margins in pixels.

If you wish to control the margins in the documents displayed in a frame you must use a style sheet.

Navigation

If you are using a framed document, there are a few differences in how navigation is managed. Usually when you click on a link, the current document, or the part of the document you are viewing is replaced by the new document you have specified. This is often not the case in a framed environment. It is common to have a list of links in a frame on the left or top of the page, which is unchanged: it is a larger central area which is updated. A typical example is shown in Figure 9.7.

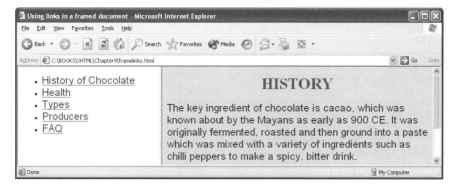

Figure 9.7 *Links in framed pages.*

The frameset document describes the allocation of space to each of the frames and names the individual frames:

```
<?xml version="1.0" encoding="ISO-8859-1"?>
<!DOCTYPE html PUBLIC "-//W3C//DTD XHTML 1.0 Frameset//EN"
"DTD/xhtml1-frameset.dtd">
<html xmlns="http://www.w3.org/1999/xhtml">
<head>
<title>Using links in a framed document</title>
<link href="linkstyle.css" type="text/css" rel="stylesheet" />
</head>
<frameset cols = "30, 70">
<frame name = "links" src = "links.html" />
<frame name = "contents" src = "contents.html" />
</frameset>
</html>
```

The document called links.html is on the left of Figure 9.7 and is a list of pointers to documents which are displayed in the frame on the right. The *anchor* elements are the same as we have seen already apart from a further attribute which specifies where the document is to be viewed:

```
<?xml version="1.0" encoding="ISO-8859-1"?>
<!DOCTYPE html PUBLIC "-//W3C//DTD XHTML 1.0 Frameset//EN"
```

```
"DTD/xhtml1-frameset.dtd">
<html xmlns="http://www.w3.org/1999/xhtml">
<head>
<link rel="stylesheet" href="linkstyle.css" type="text/css" />
<title>Left page</title>
</head>
<body>
<ul>
<li><a href="history.html" target="contents"> History of Chocolate</a></li>
<li><a href="health.html" target="contents"> Health</a></li>
<li><a href="types.html" target="contents"> Types</a></li>
<li><a href="history.html" target="contents"> Producers</a></li>
<li><a href="history.html" target="contents"> FAQ</a></li>
</ul>
</body>
</html>
```

The *target* attribute gives the name of the frame (declared in the *frame* elements of the frameset document) where the document is to be displayed when the link is clicked.

A shorthand way of achieving the same effect is to use the *base* element and the *target* attribute to give the default location for linked documents to be displayed, rather than specifying the location for every link, for example:

```
<ul>
<base target = "contents" />
<li><a href = "history.html" > History of Chocolate</a></li>
<li><a href = "health.html"> Health</a></li>
<li><a href = "types.html"> Types</a></li>
<li><a href = "history.html"> Producers</a></li>
<li><a href = "history.html"> FAQ</a></li>
</ul>
```

Special targets

In addition to specifying the target explicitly there are four special values for the *target* attribute:

- *_self*. The document is loaded into the same frame as the document which contains the link.
- *_top*. The document is loaded so that it fills the entire browser window, rather than within one of the frames.
- *_blank*. Displays the document in a new window.
- *_parent*. The document is displayed into the parent frameset of the current document. If there is no parent it is loaded into the same frame as the document containing the link, that is it has the same effect as the *_self* value for the attribute.

For example:

```
<p><a href = "history.html" target = "_top" >Whole window History</a> </p>
```

Browsers which do not support frames

Frames have been a problematic area in the past with different browsers supporting frames in different ways and many browsers either did not display frames at all or as the designer intended. To a large extent these problems have been removed: the best gifts on the Web must be the excellent browsers which can be downloaded free or at very low cost, and so users tend to upgrade frequently. The most popular browsers have supported frames for years and so even in slow moving organizations browsers which support frames are used. However, if you want your site to be available for users who do not have frame support there are a few things you can do.

The *noframes* element allows you to write some XHTML which will only be executed by browsers which do not support frames, for example:

```
<frameset cols = "30, 70">
<frame name = "links" src = "links.html" />
<frame name = "contents" src = "contents.html" />
</frameset>
<noframes>
```

```
<p>Sorry you need a browser which supports frames to see this site </p>
</noframes>
```

Rather than displaying the framed documents, the sorry message is displayed. If you do not include this, the user may simply see a blank screen. If he gets this message at least he is aware that he is not seeing the document as intended. Users who have a browser which supports frames will not see this message.

An alternative approach is to provide another web site which does not use frames, you can link to this within the *<noframes> </noframes>* pair:

```
<noframes>
    <p>Sorry you need a browser which supports frames to see this site </p>
    <p><a href = "unframed.html">Click here to go to the non-framed site</a></p>
</noframes>
```

Legal problems

You should be careful about including links to external pages in framed documents. If you have a banner header and a list of links on your site with a large contents page, you should ensure that the material which is displayed in your contents page is not copyright - if a user sees your banner and links adjacent to a major site such as CNN it implies that you own the content of that page. If you do something like this, the least you can expect is to receive a strong email telling you to change your site, at worst a legal case can be made against you. If you do link to an external site, it is safest to use the *_top* or *_blank* value for the target attribute of the link to ensure that the external document fills the entire browser or is placed in another browser window.

In-line frames

An in-line frame is sometimes called a floating frame. It is a way of displaying a document entirely within another document.

An in-line frame is produced using the *iframe* element. An example of this element is shown below:

```
<iframe name ="FAQ" src="inlineframe.html" height="50" width = "90" align = "right">
</iframe>
```

The parent document and its in-line frame are shown in Figure 9.8.

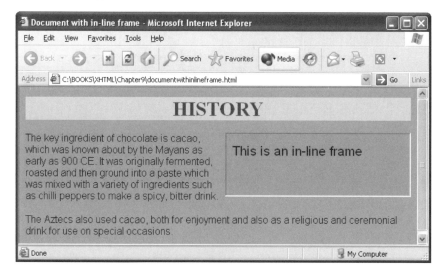

Figure 9.8 An XHTML document with an in-line frame.

The body of the document is shown below:

```
<head>
<title>Document with in-line frame</title>
<link rel="stylesheet" href="linkstyle.css" type="text/css" />
</head>
<body style ="background-color:cyan">
<h1>
```

```
HISTORY
</h1>
<iframe name = "FAQ" src="inlineframe.html" height="100" width="300"
align ="right">
<a href="inlineframe.html"></a>
</iframe>
<p>
The key ingredient of chocolate is cacao, which was known about by the Mayans as
early as 900 CE. It was originally fermented, roasted and then ground into a paste
which was mixed with a variety of ingredients such as chilli peppers to make a spicy,
bitter drink.
</p>
<p>
The Aztecs also used cacao, both for enjoyment and also as a religious and ceremonial
drink for use on special occasions.
</p>
</body>
```

The *iframe* element has all the expected attributes which we have already seen: *src, name, height, width, align* (shown in the previous example) and also *frameborder, scrolling, marginheight* and *marginwidth*.

Navigation for documents containing in-line frames is the same as for fixed frames.

Chapter

10

Creating Forms

Introduction

All of the web pages we have looked at so far have been static - that is they display a mixture of text and graphics, you can read them and click on links to go to other pages, but nothing else. If you want a more interactive page, perhaps to buy something on line, a good way of doing this is to use forms, in fact unless you use a scripting language such as JavaScript or an embedded Java applet, it is the only way in which the user can send information to the server.

Forms include all of the visual features familiar to anyone who has used any interactive computer application, text fields, lists, buttons and so on. There are a wide range of visual tools which make it easier to create forms, but they are fairly straightforward to create by typing the XHTML directly.

Creating and using forms

There are two aspects to creating and using forms:

- Creating the visual interface.
- Sending the information input to the server.

We are going to look at each of these in turn.

The form element

All of the elements of a form are placed with a *form* element, that is within a *<form> </form>* pair, placed with the body of the document, for example:

```
<body>
<form method = "post" action = "http://www.essentials/cgi-bin/pc/pcmail.txt">
... ...
</form>
</body>
```

There are two mandatory attributes for the *form* element:

- *method.*
- *action.*

It is extremely important that these two attributes are correct since they specify the method which is to be used to send the data to the server and how that data is to be processed. However, before we can look at them it is important to know what data is sent to the server by the form and to understand how forms and the controls they contain are created. We are going to do this first before looking at how form data is processed later in this chapter.

What is sent to the server?

The Common Gateway Interface (CGI) provides a smooth way of transferring data between a computer and a server. The two computers may have different configurations and operating systems, and it is the job of the CGI script on the server to receive the data and put it into a format so that it can be processed. The data sent is usually in the form of pairs of pieces of information: a name and a value, for example, if a text field called *familyname* is used to input a family name, and the name supplied is *Benelli*, the pair supplied to the server would be *familyname = Benelli*. Depending on the data which is supplied, different actions may take place, for example an email may be sent, a database may be updated or a new XHTML document may be displayed.

The basis of designing an interactive document is to create a form and add a set of controls, all of which will be familiar to anyone who has used a graphical user interface on any computer. The user makes choices by, for example, selecting items from lists, or typing text. This information is sent to the server for processing.

Controls

Controls such as buttons are the basic components which may be used in creating interactive forms. The following objects or controls as they are commonly called are available:

- Text field.
- Password field.
- Text area.
- Radio button.
- Check box.
- List.
- Buttons.

Figure 10.1 shows an example of a typical site which requests credit card details, such as the type of card, the card number, the dates between which it is valid and other essential information. This site uses typical controls such as lists and text fields.

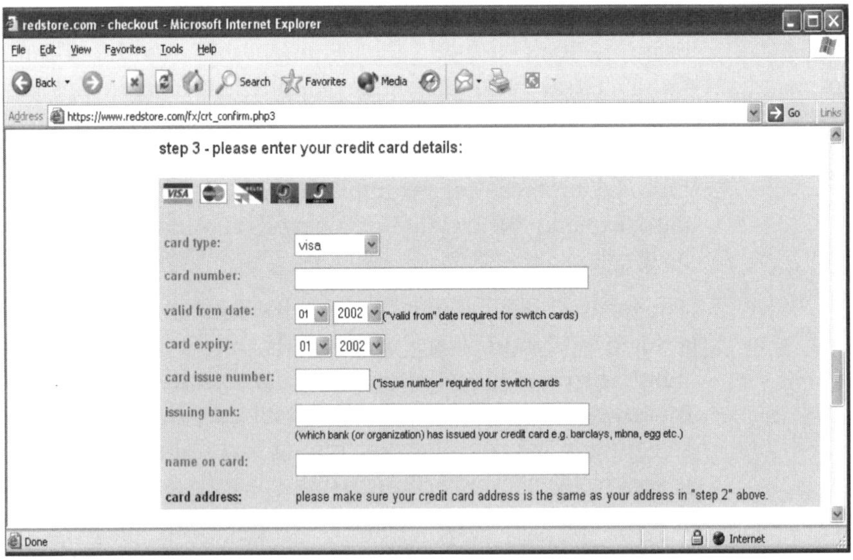

Figure 10.1 A typical page which uses controls.

The input element

The element which is used most often to display controls is the *input* element, the value of its *type* attribute determines what control is displayed.

A description of the most widely used attributes for the *input* element are shown in Table 10.1:

Table 10.1 Attributes of the *input* element.

Attribute	Description
maxlength	The maximum number of characters which can be typed in the field.
name	A name which is unique within the form and which identifies the control.
selected	The default selection when the form is first displayed.
size	The displayed size of the control.
type	The type of control, this can be either text, button, checkbox, file, hidden, image, reset or submit.
value	With controls which accept textual input such as text controls, the *value* attribute can be used to assign an initial value which is displayed when the form is first displayed. With controls which are either on/off, yes/no, such as checkboxes and radio buttons, this parameter is the text which is sent back to the server for processing if the control is checked.

The *name* attribute identifies the control to the server. There are a few simple rules about the names which can be used:

- Names cannot include spaces.
- Names are case sensitive.
- Names must be unique in the form in which they are used.

The same general guidelines for choosing names in any programming or scripting language apply:

- Names should be descriptive of the content.
- Names should be clearly unique, for example, do not use *Monday* and *Mondays* in the same form, it is very easy to confuse them.

We are going to look at displaying text fields next, that is when the value of the *type* attribute is *text*.

Text field controls

The text field control is used for inputting a single line of text. If you want to input more than one line of text the text area control should be used.

The input element is used to create a text field, the *type* attribute is assigned the value *text*. For example:

```
<p>
<input type = "text" name = "firstname" size = "25" />  First name<br />
<input type = "text" name = "familyname" size = "25" />  Family name<br />
<input type = "text" name = "AddressLine1" size = "25" />  Address line 1 <br />
<input type = "text" name = "AddressLine2" size = "25" />  Address line 2 <br />
<input type = "text" name = "Town" size = "25" />  Town<br />
<input type = "text" name = "ZipCode" size = "12" />  Zip/Postal code
</p>
```

Note that the *value* attribute is not usually given for a text field control, it is implicitly assigned the text which is typed by the user.

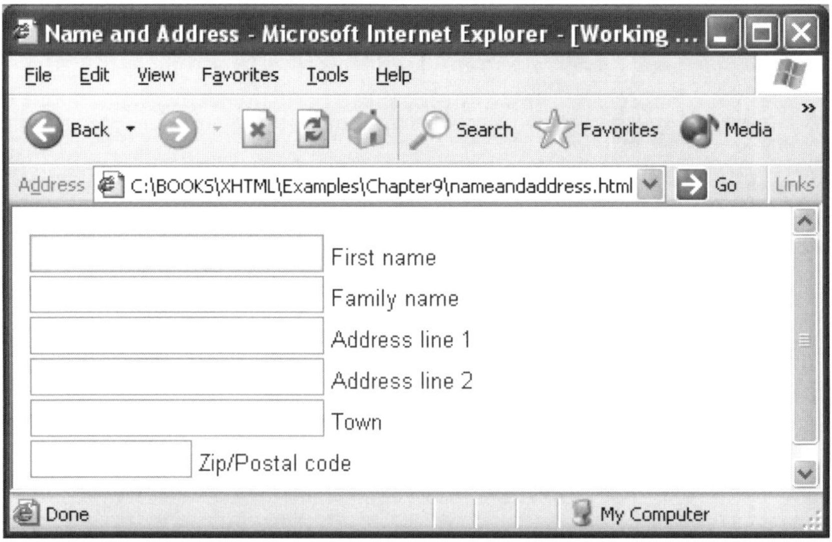

Figure 10.2 Text field controls.

This produces the text fields as shown in Figure 10.2.

It is often best to place the explanatory text on the right of the text field, so that it is lined up neatly. If this text is placed on the right of the text field it is not possible to make sure that the text fields will start in the same column, even by adding spaces to the explanatory text. In fonts which are not mono-spaced, different characters take up different amounts of space and you cannot be certain what font will be used to display the text. Mono-spaced fonts usually do not look attractive and so should not be used.

If you do not force a line break at the end of each text field and its supporting text by using the *br* element, the next control will be placed on the same line, which can look messy.

The *value* parameter can be used to provide an initial value which is displayed when the text field is first displayed, for example, if an identity code had to be input which consisted of up to 8 letters and the first was always P, the lines below could be used:

```
<p>
<input type="text" name ="IDCode" maxlength="8" size="8" value ="P" />ID code
</p>
```

This produces the text field displayed in Figure 10.3.

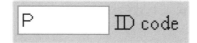

Figure 10.3 Initial text in a text field.

For both the text field and the password controls the information which is sent to the server is the control name and the text which has been input by the user.

Password controls

If the value of the *type* parameter is specified as a password, when text is typed a blob, asterisk or some other character (depending on your operating system) is displayed for every character, for example:

```
<p>
<input type = "password" name = "IDCode" maxlength="10" size="10" />Password
</p>
```

The password control produced is shown in Figure 10.4.

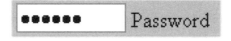

Figure 10.4 The password control.

In all other respects this control behaves in the same way as the text field.

The password control should be used with some care, since there is no encryption of the password which is typed and no validation - this is done by the server.

Checkbox controls

The checkbox control is displayed when the *type* attribute is assigned to *checkbox*. A checkbox is used to give a yes/no reply to a question, for example:

```
<p>
<input type ="checkbox" name ="forever" value = "yes" checked = "checked" />
Yes, please send me junk mail forever
</p>
```

The *checked* attribute value is given the value *checked*, so that when the checkbox is first displayed it is ticked, as shown in Figure 10.5.

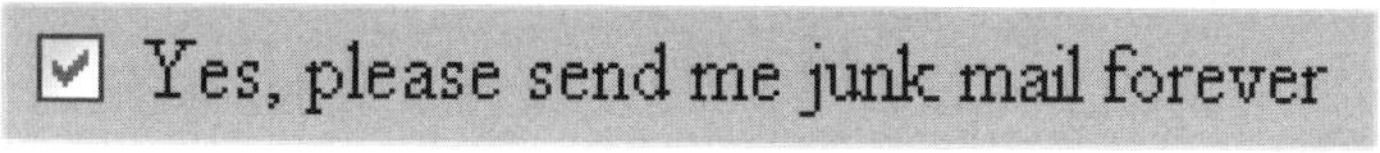

Figure 10.5 The checkbox control.

If the checkbox is checked, the name *forever* and the value *yes* are sent to the server for processing. If it is not checked, no information on this control will be sent. If the server receives no information it assumes that the control is unchecked.

Radio button controls

A radio button is displayed if the *type* attribute is *radio*. Radio button controls are similar to the checkbox controls in that you can choose one of two options by checking the control or not. The difference is that a group of radio buttons behave as a group and only one of them can be checked at any time. Checking one radio button in the group unchecks all the others, for example:

```
<p>
What's your favourite holiday destination?<br />
<input type = "radio" name ="holiday" value ="Hawaii" checked ="checked" /> Hawaii
<input type = "radio" name ="holiday" value ="Desenzano" /> Desenzano
<input type = "radio" name ="holiday" value ="Tripoli" /> Tripoli
</p>
```

This produces the radio buttons shown in Figure 10.6.

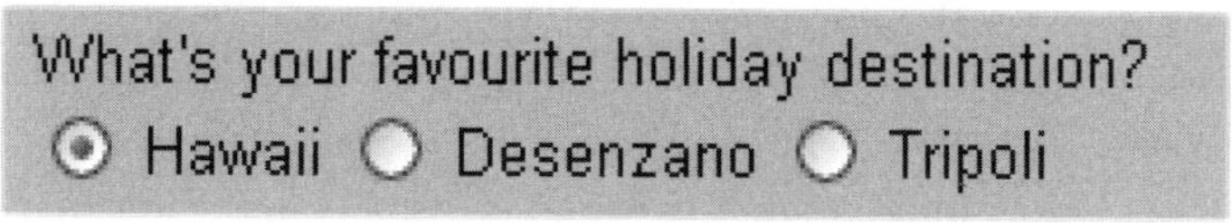

Figure 10.6 The radio button control.

Note that the *name* attribute is the same for all three of the controls, this ensures that they behave as a group. The *value* attribute specifies the text which is sent to the server for processing if that radio button is selected. For example, if *Hawaii* is checked, the name *holiday* and the value *Hawaii* are the information pair which are sent to the server. No information is sent for the radio buttons in the group which are not selected.

If one of the radio buttons has its *checked* attribute set, when they are first displayed that radio button is checked. You should only use this attribute on one of the radio buttons, since only one can be set at a time.

File input controls

A very useful control is the file input control which is displayed when the *type* attribute is assigned the value *file*, for example:

```
<input type = "file" name = "image" size = "40" maxlength = "128" />
```

It consists of two components, a text field and a button, an example is shown in Figure 10.7.

Figure 10.7 File input.

Clicking on the *Browse* button displays the open file dialog and allows you to browse through the file system of the computer. When a file is selected its name is displayed in the file input control.

The *size* attribute is the visible size of the text field. The *maxlength* attribute is the largest number of characters permitted for the file name.

You may also use the *accept* attribute, which allows you to state the MIME file types which are acceptable for download, for example:

```
<p>
<input type = "file" name = "image" size = "40" accept = "image/gif, image/jpg" />
</p>
```

will accept only GIF and JPEG files.

Buttons

There are three types of buttons, produced by using different values for the *type* attribute:

- *submit.*
- *reset.*
- *image.*

A fourth type of button can be produced by using the *button* element which we will look at later in this chapter.

The *submit* and *reset* buttons are straightforward to use, for example:

```
<p>
<input type ="submit" value ="Buy" />
<input type ="reset" value ="Clear" />
</p>
```

The two buttons produced are shown in Figure 10.8:

Figure 10.8 Button controls.

The *value* attribute is the text which is displayed on the face of the button.

The *submit* button collects the data which has been input into the form and sends it to the server in the form of name and value pairs.

The *reset* button clears all the fields and sets all selections to their default values.

You cannot control the size of a button directly, its size is determined by the text on its face (as given in the *value* attribute) - but you can make it larger by placing spaces either side of the text to approximate to the size you want.

The *image* button behaves in the same way as the *submit* button, except that an image file is used instead of a button. The *value* attribute is no longer needed as no text is displayed. Assigning the *name* attribute to *point* ensures that the co-ordinates of the mouse when the button is clicked are sent to the server for processing, along with all the other information which has been input into the form.

```
<p>
<input type ="image" name ="point" src ="buttonimage.gif" />
</p>
```

In this case a GIF file in the same folder as the form is used.

The button element

If you want to use a button to take some other action apart from submit and reset, you can use the *button* element. Buttons of this type are visually the same as buttons created using the *input* element with its *type* attribute assigned to *reset* or *submit*. The difference is that instead of carrying out a pre-defined function, you can instruct some other action to be taken when the button is clicked, by executing some scripting statements, in a language such as JavaScript, for example:

```
<button type = "button" value = "print" name = "print"
onclick = "alert('Click to print'); return true;"></button>
```

This example would display an alert box with the text *Click to print* and a single *OK* button. The events are covered in detail in Chapters 11 to 14 which deal with JavaScript and event handling.

The textarea element

A text area control is similar to a text field control. It is used for you to type text. The difference is that you can type as many times as you wish.

The *cols* and *rows* attributes allow you to specify the number of rows and columns:

```
<p>
<textarea name ="specialcomments" cols="40" rows="6">
Type any special requirements here</textarea>
</p>
```

If the display area is not large enough to show all the typed text, scrollbars are automatically added as shown in Figure 10.9.

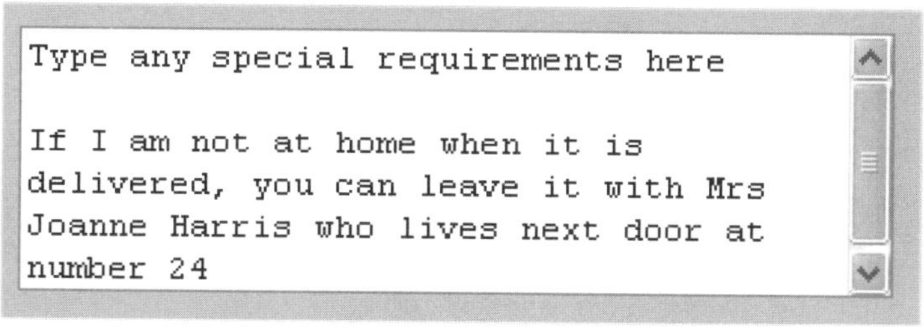

Figure 10.9 The textarea control.

The text which is initially displayed is typed after the *<textarea>* tag and before the closing *</textarea>* tag.

The *value* and *name* pair are available to be sent to the server in the same way as for a text control.

List controls

A most useful type of control is the list control - you are presented with a dropdown list of options and you can choose one of them. Where possible these controls should be used in preference to text field controls, for example when you ask a user to give his country, it is better to allow him to choose one from a list, rather than typing it. Handling freely typed text requires much more work, for example, if you live in the UK, when asked for your country you may type UK, or you may add periods, typing U.K. You may be more specific and type England, you may also use abbreviations or simply mistype. This requires a lot of work to sort out at the server end. It is much simpler if you simply allow a country to be chosen from a list.

There are two parts to creating a list:

- The *<select>* tag specifies the name of the list and other attributes for example, which control how many items may be selected.
- The *<option>* tag specifies an item which is displayed in the list.

For example:

```
<p>
<select name ="country">
<option value ="France">France</option>
<option value ="Germany">Germany</option>
<option value ="UK">UK</option>
<option value ="US">US</option>
</select>
Countries where we operate
</p>
```

This produces the drop down list as shown in Figure 10.10.

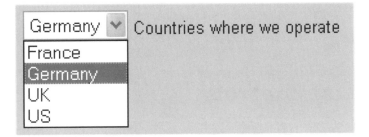

Figure 10.10 The list control.

In the *<select>* tag we have seen we relied on the default values for the attributes, but you can change these to alter the appearance and appearance of the list. Table 10.2 shows the most commonly used attributes, most of which we have already seen with other elements.

The *size* attribute has an effect on the appearance of the list box - it no longer drops down, but the number of items requested are displayed, for example, changing the *size* attribute of the previous example from the default of one to three:

Table 10.2 Attributes of the *select* element.

Attribute	Description
multiple = "multiple"	Allows multiple selection from the list.
name	A name which is unique within the form and which identifies the control.
size	The number of rows. If 1 (the default), a dropdown list is displayed.
option	An element used to insert an item in the list, one option element is required for every list item. The selected attribute of *option* is used to indicate the selected item when the list is first displayed.

```
<p>
<select name ="country" size="3">
<option value ="France">France</option>
<option value ="Germany" selected ="selected">Germany</option>
<option value ="UK">UK</option>
<option value ="US">US</option>
</select>
</p>
```

This produces the list box shown in Figure 10.11.

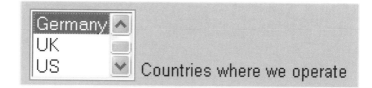

Figure 10.11 The list control with size = 3.

Note that the *selected* attribute is used for the second option attribute to make *Germany* the item which is automatically selected when the list is first displayed.

Vertical scrollbars are added automatically if all the items in the list cannot be displayed, but horizontal scrollbars are never added. The width of the list is determined by the length of the longest item in the list.

By using the *multiple* attribute, you can allow more than one item to be selected, for example:

```
<select name ="country" size="4" multiple = "multiple">
```

This produces the list shown in Figure 10.12.

Figure 10.12 Multiple selection from lists.

More than one item may be selected in two ways: select one item by clicking on it and then others by clicking on them with the Ctrl key pressed; or you can select a range of items by first selecting one item and then another with the Shift key pressed, all items between this pair are selected. It is not possible to limit how many items may be selected.

When information on selected items is submitted to the server, the name specified in the *<select>* tag is used and the value of the selected item.

Grouping controls

A useful way of grouping controls is to use the *legend* and *fieldset* elements, which places a box and optional title around controls.

The controls to be grouped are placed within a *<fieldset>* and *</fieldset>* pair. The opening *<fieldset>* tag is followed by a *<legend>* tag:

```
<fieldset>
     <legend>The title</legend>
     ......
</fieldset>
```

An example of these elements is shown below.

```
<fieldset>
<legend>Extras</legend>
Extras are also available<br />
<input type ="checkbox" name ="dvd" value ="dvd" />
DVD writer - add $20
<input type ="checkbox" name ="Broadband" value ="broadband" />
Broadband ready - add $60
<input type ="checkbox" name ="flat17screen" value="flat17screen" />
Flat 17" screen - add $120
</fieldset>
```

The output is shown in Figure 10.13.

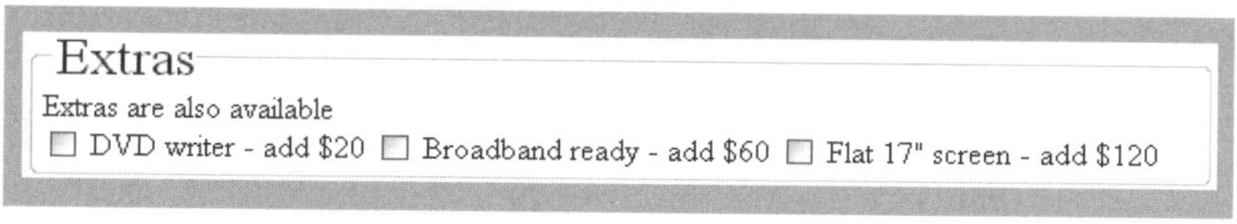

Figure 10.13 The fieldset and legend elements.

Disabling controls

There are two ways of disabling controls so that you can see them, but cannot write or use them. For controls such as text fields where you write text you can use either the *readonly* or the *disabled* attributes, for example:

```
<input type = "text" name = "familyname" readonly = "readonly"/> Family name
```

The control is visible but nothing can be typed into it.

For controls where a choice is made from a list, rather than by typing, the *disabled* attribute should be used, for example:

```
<select name = "country" size = "4" disabled = "disabled">
```

The PC buyer document

We have seen the individual controls in action, but it is helpful to see how they can be combined to provide an attractive document, in this case for ordering a PC.

The completed document is shown in Figure 10.14.

This document uses most of the controls we have seen to allow all the information required to indicate the specification of the PC required and the name and address details of the user.

A style sheet is used to specify the characteristics of the fonts used and to ensure a consistent look to the document. If other documents are created for the site, the same style sheet can be used to give a professional appearance. Customers will not want to spend money with a company that has an amateur looking Web site.

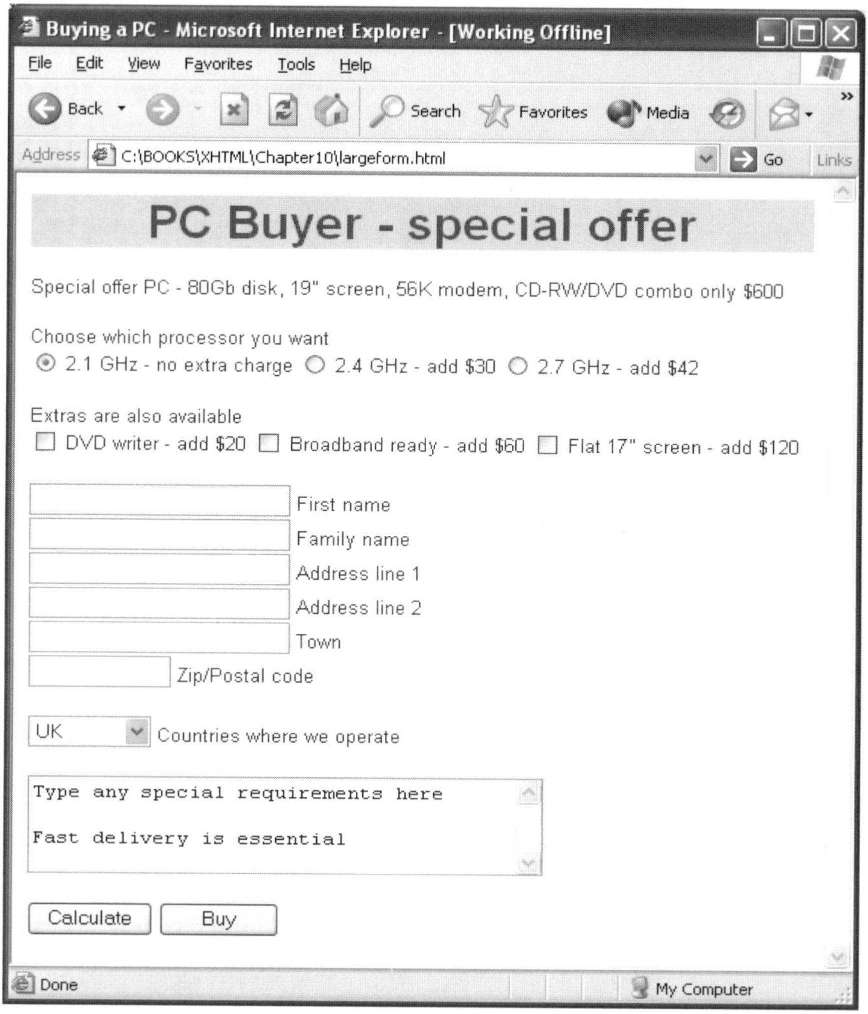

Figure 10.14 The PC buyer form.

The complete listing for the XHTML used to produce this page is shown below:

```
<?xml version = "1.0" encoding = "ISO-8859-1"?>
<!DOCTYPE html PUBLIC "-//W3C//DTD XHTML 1.0 Strict//EN"
"http://www.w3.org/TR/xhtml1/DTD/xhtml1-strict.dtd">
<html xmlns = "http://www.w3.org/1999/xhtml">
<head>
<title>Buying a PC</title>
```

```
<link rel = "stylesheet" href = "mystyle.css" type = "text/css" />
</head>
<body>
<form method = "post" action = "http://www.essentials/cgi-bin/pc/pcmail.txt">
<h1>PC Buyer - special offer</h1>
<p>
Special offer PC - 80Gb disk, 19" screen, 56K modem, CD-RW/DVD combo only $600
</p>
<p>
Choose which processor you want<br />
<input type = "radio" name = "cpu" value = "2.1" checked = "checked" />
 2.1 GHz - no extra charge
<input type = "radio" name = "cpu" value = "2.4" />
 2.4 GHz - add $30
<input type = "radio" name = "cpu" value = "2.7" />
 2.7 GHz - add $42
</p>
<p>
Extras are also available<br />
<input type = "checkbox" name = "dvd" value = "dvd" />
 DVD writer - add $20
<input type = "checkbox" name = "Broadband" value = "broadband" />
 Broadband ready - add $60
<input type = "checkbox" name = "flat17screen" value = "flat17screen" />
 Flat 17" screen - add $120
</p>
<p>
<input type = "text" name = "firstname" size = "25" /> First name<br />
<input type = "text" name = "familyname" size = "25" /> Family name<br />
<input type = "text" name = "AddressLine1" size = "25" /> Address line 1 <br />
<input type = "text" name = "AddressLine2" size = "25" /> Address line 2 <br />
<input type = "text" name = "Town" size = "25" /> Town<br />
<input type = "text" name = "ZipCode" size = "12" /> Zip/Postal code
</p>
<p>
<select name = "country">
<option value = "France">France</option>
<option value = "Germany">Germany</option>
<option value = "UK">UK</option>
<option value = "US">US</option>
</select>
Countries where we operate
```

```
</p>
<p>
<textarea name = "specialcomments" cols = "40" rows = "4">
Type any special requirements here</textarea>
</p>
<p>
<input type = "submit" value = "Calculate" />
<input type = "submit" value = "    Buy    " />
</p>
</form>
</body>
</html>
```

An important aspect of a page is the spacing between different parts of the page. In this example, the separate items are placed in paragraphs, using the *p* element.

The browser will simply place one control alongside the previous control if there is room. This can look messy and give unpredictable results, therefore it is a good idea to be explicit about where line breaks come and to use the *br* element to do this.

The radio buttons and the checkboxes have been placed on one line to save space and to ensure that the whole of the document fits onto a typical screen.

Spaces are added to the label on the *Buy* button so that it is about the same width as the *Calculate* button.

Processing forms

When a form has been completed its contents must be sent to the server for processing. The data is always sent as a set of name-value pairs. The name identifies the control. The value gives the state of the control, for example, whether a checkbox is checked or not, or which item has been selected from a list. The server can handle the information in three ways:

• Write the data to a file or database.

- Read data from a database using the form data as the basis of a query.
- Email the data elsewhere.

The method used is based partly on how you want to process the data, and also on the configuration of your server. It is important to discuss with the manager of your server what is available for processing form data.

If you have a large volume of data the best way to deal with the results is to enter them into a database. This can be done without any intervention and the results processed by using straightforward SQL queries.

The simplest solution is to create an email containing the data, the only problem with this approach is that the processing requires more work. If you only have a hundred emails this is not too difficult to handle, but as the numbers grow the processing becomes more onerous and it is best to go for the database solution.

You specify what action is to be taken by the server by using the *<form>* tag and its *method* and *action* attributes.

The form element

The *<form>* and *</form>* tags enclose all of the controls in the form.

The *<form>* tag has two attributes, *method* and *action*, which you must include:

- The *method* attribute. This can be either *post* or *get* and indicates how the data is to be sent to the server.
- The *action* attribute. This is the name and path of the script which will process the data.

The method attribute

There are two possible ways in which data can be sent to the server, either as part of a URL, (*method = "get"*) or in a separate file (*method = "post"*).

The value *get* is used when there is not very much data to send. There is a limit of 1024 characters on the maximum size of a URL. There may also be a security problem, since URLs are often saved by ISPs, and if the URL contains sensitive data it is also saved.

The value *post* is usually the preferred way because it does not have these limitations, the file may be of any length and is destroyed after it has been received and processed.

The action attribute

This attribute gives the name and full path of the script which processes the data, scripts are usually stored in a folder called cgi-bin. An example of the *<form>* tag shows what both the *method* and *action* attributes might be:

```
<form method = "post" action = "http://www.essentials/cgi-bin/pc/pcmail.txt">
```

You will need to speak to your server manager to know where you can place your processing scripts on your system.

Using email to process a form

To create an email from a form, you need an application which is able to read the data sent from the form and generate an email. A popular and widely used form-to-email application for a PC is called MailPost which is available from http://www.mcenter.com/mail/post. If you are using Unix, similar applications such as cgiemail are available and are functionally virtually identical.

Setting the form element

The first stage is to set the *action* and *method* attributes of the *<form>* tag correctly, as we are sending an email, the method attribute is *post*. The *action* attribute is assigned to the address of the email template document, for example:

```
<form method = "post" action = "http://www.essentials/cgi-bin/pc/pcmail.txt
```

The *</form>* tag must be placed after all of the controls to close the *form* element.

Creating the template document

The second stage is to create an email template document, this is a text file which has text with the values of the controls placed so that the email makes sense, for example, if we had two text fields for the user's name:

```
<input type = "text" name = "firstname" size = "25" /> First name<br />
<input type = "text" name = "familyname" size = "25" /> Family name<br />
```

a part of the email template could be:

```
Welcome [firstname] [familyname].
```

The items in brackets refer to the *name* attribute in the *<input>* tag. When the email is sent, these items are replaced with the name which has been typed, so for the input shown in Figure 10.15, this part of the email would be:

```
Welcome Sally Vickers.
```

Figure 10.15 Getting data from the form.

For the PC buyer application shown in Figure 10.14, the following template would be suitable:

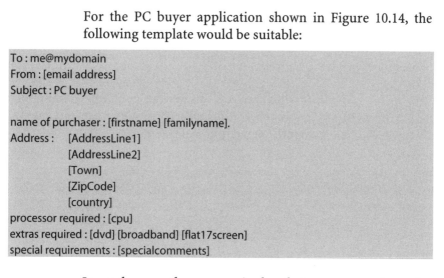

```
To : me@mydomain
From : [email address]
Subject : PC buyer

name of purchaser : [firstname] [familyname].
Address :    [AddressLine1]
             [AddressLine2]
             [Town]
             [ZipCode]
             [country]
processor required : [cpu]
extras required : [dvd] [broadband] [flat17screen]
special requirements : [specialcomments]
```

In each case the names in brackets correspond to the control names in the XHTML file. When the email is sent, the values inserted could be, for example, the text typed into a text field, some text indicating that a radio button has been checked or a particular list item selected.

In this case the *from* email address is where the email originates from, if you were sending a confirmation of order, you could use an email supplied by the user.

This application has some useful features, if for example, you wanted to insist that the user put their name on the form you could do this by adding the prefix *required* to the XHTML form and also to the email template, for example, the XHTML line becomes:

```
<input type = "text" name = "required-firstname" size = "25" />  First name<br />
<input type = "text" name = "required-familyname" size = "25" />  Family name<br />
```

The line in the template becomes:

```
name of purchaser : [required-firstname] [required-familyname].
```

If a required field is not supplied the form is rejected.

This Form-to-Email application also has a useful facility which allows you to test your XHTML and template without actually sending the document, by adding the following line to your XHTML:

```
<input type = "hidden" name - "*nosend*">
```

MailPost will allow you to see what your email would look like if it was sent. If it looks correct you can remove this line so that the email is actually sent.

Chapter

11

JavaScript and XHTML

Introduction

JavaScript is most commonly embedded within an XHTML Web page to provide additional features which are not available simply through using XHTML alone. For JavaScript-enhanced Web pages to behave correctly, the browser used to view it must have a JavaScript interpreter. There are still some die-hards who are not using JavaScript enabled versions of these browsers, but since browsers can be downloaded free, the vast majority of users can be assumed to have browsers which will interpret the latest versions of JavaScript correctly. A more serious problem is that the JavaScript interpreters in the two leading browsers from Netscape and Microsoft either do not understand all of the features of JavaScript or interpret them in different ways. JavaScript and the browsers are constantly evolving and if you are developing applications using JavaScript it is advisable to check that the final version works with a variety of popular browsers. The picture is further complicated by other scripting languages such as Microsoft's JScript which is very similar to JavaScript.

JavaScript which is interpreted by a browser is called client-side JavaScript. There are several ways in which JavaScript can be connected to XHTML documents which we are going to look at in this chapter.

JavaScript should not be confused with the Java programming language - although both can be used to enhance your Web pages. We are not going to look at how to create Java programs, only how to incorporate them into your Web pages.

Java and JavaScript

Java is a general purpose object-oriented programming language which may be used for a wide range of applications. It has an extensive set of supporting class libraries, which among other facilities, allow you to reference files and databases to create user interfaces, multi-threaded applications and components. A widely used category of Java applications are called applets, these can run within a Web browser environment.

Using Java applets

One or more Java source files are compiled to produce class files. It is these class files which are executed by the browser. There are two elements which may be used to specify the Java class file. The *applet* element is very widely used, and although this is deprecated in XHTML the Transitional DTD supports it. The alternative is to use the *object* element. The *applet* element is specifically used to incorporate Java applets into a Web page, while the *object* element has a more general role and can be used to include any software object.

The simplest form of the *applet* element has only one attribute which gives the name of the class file, for example:

```
<applet code = "scribble.class">
</applet>
```

When the opening tag is reached, the applet is run. When it completes, the XHTML tags which follow are executed.

The *applet* and *object* elements share the attributes shown in Table 11.1.

The *object* element is used in a similar way except that the *classid* attribute is used instead of the *code* attribute to specify the Java applet.

Table 11.1 Attributes of the *applet* and *object* elements.

Attribute	Description
align	Specifies the alignment as *left*| *right*| *centertexttop*| *middle*| *textmiddle*| *baseline*| or *textbottom*. Now deprecated in favour of using style sheets.
archive	A list of URLs separated by commas which should be pre-loaded to improve performance.
class	The name of the class file to be run.
codebase	The folder containing the required files.
height	The height of the area in pixels allocated to the applet.
hspace	The white space in pixels to the left and right of the applet.
id	Assigns an identifier to the applet so that it can be referenced.
name	Specifies a name for the applet so that it can be referenced.
style	Specifies layout information.
title	Specifies a title to the element.
vspace	The white space in pixels above and below the applet.
width	The width of the area in pixels allocatted to the applet.

In addition to the attributes listed in Table 11.1, the *object* element has some further attributes listed in Table 11.2.

Table 11.2 Attributes of the *object* element.

Attribute	Description
border	The border width around the object. This is deprecated in favour of style sheets.
codetype	The content type of the object's code.
data	A URL giving the location of the object's data.
declare	Defines the object, but does not load it.
standby	Specifies a message which the browser displays while the object is loading.
tabindex	The tabbing position of the object.

In the example shown below, the *object* element is used with its *classid, name, width* and *height* attributes. The applet produced is shown in Figure 11.1. The scribble applet tracks mouse movement and reproduces it in the applet window.

```
<body>
<h1>Using a Java applet</h1>
<p>
<object classid = "java:scribble.class"
```

```
name ="scribble"
width="500"
height="150" >
</object>
</p>
```

The *param* element may be used with both the *applet* and *object* tags to pass information from the XHTML file to the Java applet, for example:

```
<object classid = "java:scribble.class"
name ="scribble"
width="500"
height="150" >
<param name ="chocolate" value="1" />
<param name ="cake" value ="true" />
</object>
```

The applet will require some Java code to receive this data.

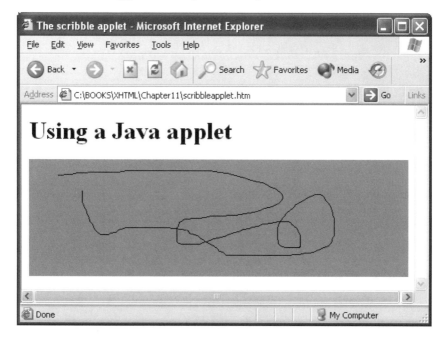

Figure 11.1 Embedding a Java applet within XHTML.

Using JavaScript

JavaScript code is placed within the *script* element. An example of a single line of JavaScript within an XHTML document produces the page shown in Figure 11.2.

Figure 11.2 Embedding JavaScript within XHTML.

The document which produces this page is:

```
<?xml version="1.0" encoding="ISO-8859-1"?>
<!DOCTYPE html PUBLIC "-//W3C//DTD XHTML 1.0 Strict//EN"
"http://www.w3.org/TR/xhtml1/DTD/xhtml1-strict.dtd">
<html xmlns="http://www.w3.org/1999/xhtml">
<head>
<title>Using JavaScript in XHTML</title>
<link rel="stylesheet" href="mystyle.css" type="text/css" />
</head>
<body>
<h1>
<script type = "text/javascript">
<!--
document.write("My first line of JavaScript");
// -->
</script>
</h1>
</body>
</html>
```

If you look closely at the previous example you will see that the JavaScript is placed within an XHTML comment, that is, it is placed within a block which starts with <!-- and ends with the characters -->. This ensures that the JavaScript is ignored by the browser which is fooled into thinking that it is just comment and can be ignored.

A further problem is that the closing --> must be hidden from the JavaScript interpreter. This is done by adding the // characters at the start of the line which contains these characters.

You need to do this every time you insert some JavaScript into your document. Immediately after the opening *<script>* tag insert the <!-- and immediately before the closing *</script>* tag insert // -->, for example:

```
<script language = "JavaScript">
//<!-- this line fools old browsers into thinking that the JavaScript is HTML comment
        document.write ("My first line of JavaScript")
// this is the end of the JavaScript and the end of the XHTML comment -->
</script>
```

The two most commonly used attributes of the *<script>* tag are:

- *type.*
- *src.*

We are going to look at both of these.

The type attribute

The *<script>* tag has a *type* attribute which specifies which scripting language is being used, for example:

```
<script type = "text/javascript">
```

This specifies that the browser must support JavaScript. If it does not, the JavaScript will be ignored.

The end of the scripting code is specified by the *</script>* tag.

The src attribute

The *src* attribute in a *<script>* tag allows you to specify a file which contains lines of JavaScript rather than embedding these lines directly within the XHTML, for example:

```
<script src ="hi.js" type = "text/javascript">
```

The file should have an extension of .js and does not contain any XHTML, in particular the *</script>* tag must remain in the XHTML document, since any browser which does not understand JavaScript will ignore any code until it reaches this element.

It is good practice to use the *src* attribute because:

- Some lines of JavaScript may be used in more than one place in an application. Placing these lines in a file means that changes only have to be made in one place and maintenance is therefore easier.
- The speed of response is improved since the JavaScript file may be cached the first time it is used and therefore available without disk activity on subsequent occasions when it is needed.
- The XHTML file is reduced in length and is therefore easier to debug.

The CDATA Section

The technique of making JavaScript a comment to hide it from browsers which do not understand JavaScript is not the preferred way of incorporating scripts into an XHTML document according to the XHTML specification. The recommended method is to use a CDATA section, this has the form:

```
<script>
<![CDATA[
```

```
......script goes here
]]>
</script>
```

Unfortunately this is not supported by most current browsers and so you have little alternative but to make your JavaScript into an XHTML comment.

An alternative approach which is future-proofed is to place all of your JavaScript into a separate file using the *src* attribute of the *<script>* tag.

JavaScript data types

JavaScript supports only three data types, numbers, strings and booleans, unlike most programming languages which have a far more extensive set.

In addition to the basic data types Java supports two abstract data types, objects and arrays. JavaScript also allows you to use functions as data types .

Identifiers

Identifiers are the names of variables, functions and labels. There are a few rules which specify the form which names can take.

- The first character must be an upper or lower case ASCII letter(a→z, A→Z), an underscore character (_)or a dollar sign ($).
- Subsequent characters may be any or the above and in addition numbers(0→9).
- Spaces are not allowed.
- Identifiers must not be the same as any JavaScript reserved word. A list of reserved words is shown in Table 11.3.

The following are valid identifier names:

```
ThisIsAVeryLongVariableName
c
_3InTheMorning
$hetty
```

Table 11.3 JavaScript reserved words.

abstract	boolean	break	byte	case	catch	char
class	const	continue	debugger	default	delete	do
double	else	enum	export	extends	false	final
finally	float	for	function	goto	if	implements
import	instanceof	in	int	interface	long	native
new	null	private	package	protected	public	return
short	static	super	switch	synchronized	this	throw
throws	transient	true	try	typeof	var	void
colatile	while	with				

Numbers

JavaScript does not make any distinction between integer and floating point numbers. All numbers are stored in floating point format. The largest value which can be represented is $\pm 1.8 \times 10^{308}$. The smallest value which can be represented is $\pm 5 \times 10^{-324}$. This format corresponds to the double data type in Java.

You can specify numbers directly in JavaScript, these are called literals.

Integer literals

Integer literals between $\pm 2^{53}$ (± 9007199254740992) can be represented exactly, you can represent large values, however these may not be exactly stored, since all numbers are stored in a floating point format. Some examples are given below:

```
0
126785965
-23876
```

Note that integer literals may not start with zero followed by a sequence of digits. A leading zero indicates an octal literal.

Floating point literals

Floating point literals can be represented in scientific notation, that is with the letter 'e' or 'E' followed by an integer exponent up to three digits long. For example:

```
0.2943
.7893
-1.34e-83
```

Strictly speaking the negative sign in front of a literal is a negation operator – and not a part of the literal itself.

Octal and hexadecimal literals

The third and final type of numeric literal is for octal and hexadecimal numbers. Octal numbers have a radix of 8, therefore octal numbers only have the digits 0→7. Hexadecimal numbers have a radix of 16, each of these 16 digits is represented by digits in the range 0→9 and A→F, that is the hexadecimal digit A represents the decimal number 10 and so on.

To indicate an octal number, place the digit zero in front of the digits. Similarly to indicate a hexadecimal number the sequence of digits is preceded by 0x or 0X. For example:

```
074
0736
0xff34ed
```

```
0x56EA93
0X3BA67
```

You can carry out operations using numeric variables and literals. In the next section we are going to look at the arithmetic operators.

Arithmetic operators

JavaScript has a similar set of operators to most programming languages, but there may be one or two surprises because of the unusual way in which JavaScript stores its numeric data – in floating point format. The arithmetic operators are listed in Table 11.4.

Table 11.4 The arithmetic operators.

Operator	Meaning
+	plus
-	subtract
*	multiply
/	divide
%	modulus
-	negation

The divide operator always gives a floating point result, for example 7/3 gives 3.5 not 3.

The modulus operator gives the remainder after division, for example 7%3 gives 1. This can be used with non-integers, for example 1.1 % 0.3 gives 0.2

The negation operator converts a positive value to a negative value and vice-versa, for example –3.7.

Increment & decrement

Among the most common operations that are carried out on numbers is to increment or decrement them and

JavaScript in common with Java has two special operators which do this as shown in Table 11.5.

Table 11.5 The increment and decrement operators.

Operator	Meaning
++	add one
--	subtract one

These operators can be placed either before or after a variable, for example:

```
++c;
c++;
```

In this case the lines do the same thing. In the next example, the value of c is incremented from 2 to 3 and then assigned to d, so both c and d have the value 3.

```
c = 2;
d = ++c;
```

If we place the increment operator after the variable, for example:

```
c = 2;
d = c++;
```

the increment is done after the assignment, so d has the value 2 and c the value 3.

The decrement operator behaves in the same way.

Shortcut operators

Operations such as:

```
c = c + 7;
```

are very common in programming and JavaScript has a shorthand way of doing this. The statement:

```
c += 7;
```

has the same effect. Similarly, there are shortcut operators for the other basic mathematical operations as shown in Table 11.6.

Table 11.6 The shortcut operators.

Operator	Example	Meaning	Value if c = 25
+ =	c + = 7;	c = c + 7;	32
-- =	c - = 3;	c = c - 3;	22
* =	c * = 5;	c = c * 5;	125
/ =	c / = 4;	c = c / 4;	6.25
% =	c % = 7	c = % 7	4

Strings

A string is a sequence of zero or more characters enclosed in either single or double quotes. There is no char data type as in languages such as Java. A single character is simply a string of length one. For example:

```
'this is a string'
"this is also a string"
"He said 'Buy me some chocolate' "
```

The only feature which might catch you out is that you can use the single quote character within strings delimited by double quotes, and also the double quotes within strings delimited by single quotes.

Escape sequences

There are some characters which you cannot type directly into a string literal, for example a backspace character. There is a special notation which allows you to display these characters as shown in Table 11.7.

Table 11.7 Escape sequences.

Sequence	Meaning
\b	Backspace.
\f	Form feed.
\n	New line.
\t	Tab.
\'	Single quote.
\"	Double quote.
\\	Backslash.
\XXX	XXX is an octal number. The character displayed corresponds to the 8 bit Latin-1 encoding. XXX must be between 0 and 377, e.g. \765.
\xXX	XX is a hexadecimal number. The character displayed correcponds to the 8-bit Latin-1 encoding. XX must be between 0 and FF, e.g. \xF6.

If the \ precedes any other character not in the table it is ignored, for example '\a' is interpreted as 'a'.

Working with strings

The + operator can also be applied to strings, for example:

```
weather = "It's a hot day " + "I hope it's not global warming"
```

The plus operator concatenates the strings.

If this operator is applied to one string and one number, the number is converted into a string and the two are concatenated.

```
a = "2" + "3";
b = "2" + 3;
```

In both of the above cases the result produced is the string "23" not the number 5.

Booleans

A boolean value has only one of two values, true or false, for example:

```
male = true;
```

booleans should be used for storing quantities which can have only two values, for example male/female, on/off, student/non-student.

Functions

If there is a particular sequence of program instructions that you are going to use more than once, those lines can be placed within a function and that function can be called wherever you want to use it. A function is a block of code which starts with the reserved word function and encloses the lines of code within a { } as shown. In the next example, the function is called *hi*. It is passed the name of a person and displays the message *Hello* followed by the person's name.

```
<head>
<title>Saying Hello</title>
</head>
<body>
<h1>
<script type = "text/javascript">
<!--
function hi(name) {
document.write("hello   " + name);
}
hi("Bill")              //call the hi function
hi("Sally")             //call it again
// -->
</script>
</h1>
</body>
```

This displays the Web page shown in Figure 11.3. We will see in the next section how to put the two messages on different lines.

When the application runs, the function is not executed until it is called by specifying the name of the function and a string literal which is passed to it. A function can be called as many times as required.

Figure 11.3 The hi function.

If you wish to use this JavaScript function in more than one document you can place it into a file with a .js extension, in this case the file has been called hi.js and is in the same folder as the XHTML document:

```
function hi(name) {
document.write("hello " + name)
}
```

The XHTML document becomes:

```
<head>
<title>Saying Hello</title>
</head>
<body>
<h1>
<script src ="hi.js" type = "text/javascript">
</script>
<script type = "text/javascript">
<!--
hi("Bill")              //call the hi function
hi("Sally")             //call it again
// -->
</script>
```

```
</h1>
</body>
```

write and writeln

There is a *writeln* method which can be used in place of the *write* method. This method does exactly the same except that it adds a newline after the text is printed. However, if you substitute *writeln* for *write*, you will find that it makes no difference to the document displayed in the browser. This is because XHTML ignores line break characters. If you were writing to a text file, *writeln* would have the expected result. If you want to amend the previous example to display the two hello messages on different lines you could use another *write* statement to print the XHTML *br* element:

```
function hi(name) {
document.write("hello   " + name);
document.write("<br />");
}
```

Passing more than one value

Sometimes you may need to pass more than one value to a function and perhaps return a value.

The *area* function shown below is passed three number variables. The surface area of the box is calculated and the result is passed back in the *return* statement.

```
<body>
<h1>
<script type = "text/javascript">
<!--
function area(len, height, width) {
theArea = 2*(height * len + height *
width + len * width);
```

```
return theArea;
}
boxArea = area(2,3,4);              //call the area function
document.write("The box surface area is " + boxArea);
// -->
</script>
</h1>
</body>
```

The running application is shown in Figure 11.4.

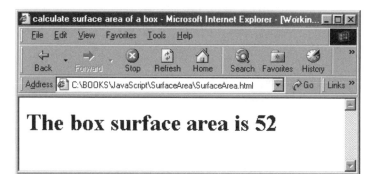

Figure 11.4 *The area function.*

Scope of variables

If you tried some of the earlier examples, you probably just started using the variables without declaring them. This appears to work, but the variables you created had global scope, that is they were available throughout your entire JavaScript application. If you wish to limit the scope of a variable you must declare it within the function in which it is used. It is then only available within that function and is said to have local scope. It is good programming practice to limit the scope of variables as much as possible. This is done by declaring variables:

- Variables declared in a function have local scope.

- Variables which are declared outside a function or which are not declared have global scope.

Unlike Java there is no block scope for variables.

Declaring variables

Before a variable can be used in JavaScript it must be defined. You do this by using the reserved word *var* and following it by the variables you want to declare, for example:

```
var c;
var count = 0, d = 0, myName;
var theDay = "Wednesday";
```

you can declare one or more variables on the same line and also initialize one or more of them.

A common error occurs when a local and global variable are given the same name. In these cases if a local and global variable are both available the one referenced is the local variable.

What's next?

In this chapter we have looked at some of the key aspects of JavaScript. In the next we are going to look at the syntax of JavaScript and how it can be used to enhance your XHTML documents.

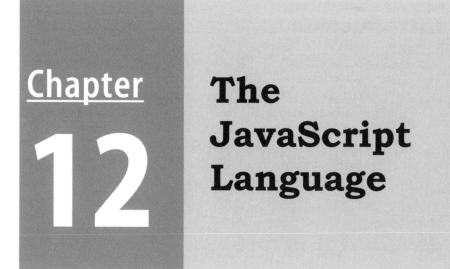

Chapter 12

The JavaScript Language

Introduction

We have seen in the previous chapter how to embed JavaScript into HTML and how JavaScript defines and uses data. In this chapter we are going to look at the format of JavaScript statements and the key groups of JavaScript statements: the branching statements which allow applications to make decisions on the basis of data and the looping statements which allow a program to execute the same block of code many times.

JavaScript errors

One of the problems that you will find when you start writing JavaScript is that if you make a mistake, the browser may show the document incorrectly or even a blank screen and it can be difficult to find out where the problem is. I have found that the best way to developing software is to adopt an incremental approach: that is to get a very basic form of the application working and then to extend it - taking a copy at every stage, so that you can go back to the previous working version should disaster happen and you cannot find the problem with your current version. This sort of approach is sometimes not well regarded by more traditional programmers, but it is being widely adopted by the new range of lightweight, agile software development paradigms such as XP or eXtreme Programming which advocates this incremental approach.

Formatting JavaScript code

JavaScript ignores white space in lines of code; you can place spaces, tabs and line breaks anywhere within a line of code between the separate items or tokens of the line. Most

JavaScript programmers use the usual programming conventions of indenting code when using branching or looping constructs to aid readability.

There is an optional semicolon(;) after each line of JavaScript. It does not matter if you omit the semicolon unless you wish to place more than one program statement on a line, for example;

```
c = 0;       d = 0;     e = 0;
```

In this case the semicolons are mandatory to avoid a syntax error. It is not considered good practice to have more than one statement on a line, since it can reduce readability.

Comments

There are two ways of adding comments to JavaScript. The // characters indicate that any text after them up to the end of the line are comment.

If you want more than one line of comments you can use /* to start the comment and */ to end it, for example:

```
// This is a single line of comment
       c = 0;        //this is comment too
/*     this is the start
       of several lines of comment
*/
```

Case sensitivity

JavaScript is case sensitive, that is reserved words such as *return* must be typed exactly as shown. A common source of error is to confuse the case of variables. A variable called *theAnswer* is not the same as *TheAnswer* or *Theanswer*.

Compound statements

If you want to group a number of program statements together so that they behave as a single unit, you can enclose them in a { } pair. We have already seen this in action in functions. The { character marks the start of the body of the function and the } marks its end. Anywhere that you can use a single statement you can use a compound statement.

The *if* statement

The *if* statement allows your program to do different things depending on the value of data. The basic form of this statement is:

```
if (expression)
      statement
```

In the example a check is made to determine the name of the browser being used to view the page, *navigator* is the name of a JavaScript object and *appName* is the property of the object that identifies the browser name.

```
<script type = "text/javascript">
<!--
var browserType;
browserType = navigator.appName      //returns the name of your browser
if (browserType == "Microsoft Internet Explorer") {
      document.write("You are running Internet Explorer");
      }
// -->
</script>
```

If the browser being used is Internet Explorer the message You are running Internet Explorer is displayed.

Note that the comparison operator == is used to test for equality. The operator = is used for assignment. The result of this test is a boolean, that is either a true or false value. If the two quantities are equal, true is produced and the following statement is executed.

If you want to execute more than one line when the condition is met, you can use a compound statement:

```
if (expression) {
        statement                    //as many statements as you wish
        statement
        ....
}
```

and we could change our application to:

```
<script type = "text/javascript">
<!--
var browserType;
browserType = navigator.appName      //returns the name of your browser
if (browserType == "Microsoft Internet Explorer") {
        document.write("You are running Internet Explorer");
        document.write("<br />");
        document.write("I hope it's version 6.2 or later");
        }
// -->
</script>
```

When it is viewed with Internet Explorer the page shown in Figure 12.1 is displayed.

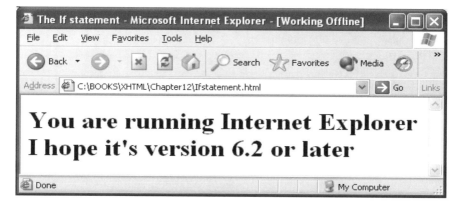

Figure 12.1 Using if statements.

Other browsers will not display anything.

The *else* clause

Sometimes you may want to take one action if a condition is met and another if it is not. You can do this by adding an *else* clause to the *if* statement. This has the basic form:

```
if (expression)
      statement
else
      statement
```

or in its compound form:

```
if (expression) {
      statement
      statement
      ...
      }
else   {
      statement
      statement
      ...
      }
```

For example, we can add an *else if* clause to our application as shown:

```
<script type = "text/javascript">
<!--
var browserType;
browserType = navigator.appName      //returns the name of your browser
      if (browserType == "Microsoft Internet Explorer") {
            document.write("Your are running Internet Explorer");
            document.write ("<br />");
            document.write("I hope it's version 6.2 or later");
            }
      else if (browserType == "Netscape") {
            document.write("You are running Netscape Navigator");
            document.write ("<br />");
            document.write("I hope it's version 6.3 or later");
```

```
        }
// -->
</script>
```

The *else if* clause

The *if* statement can be extended even further, with the addition of more *else if* clauses as shown:

```
<script type = "text/javascript">
<!--
var browserType;
browserType = navigator.appName      //returns the name of your browser
     if (browserType == "Microsoft Internet Explorer") {
            document.write("Your are running Internet Explorer");
            document.write ("<br />");
            document.write("I hope it's version 6.2 or later");
            }
     else if (browserType == "Netscape") {
            document.write("You are running Netscape Navigator");
            document.write ("<br />");
            document.write("I hope it's version 6.3 or later");
            }
     else {
            document.write("You are not running Netscape or Explorer");
            document.write("<br />");
            document.write("I wonder why not?");
            }
// -->
</script>
```

The navigator object is used to identify what browser is being used, we look at the navigator in detail in the next chapter. In this example, different messages are displayed if the browser is Internet Explorer or Netscape Navigator. If neither of these browsers is being used, the third message is displayed. Figure 12.2 shows the page displayed by Netscape.

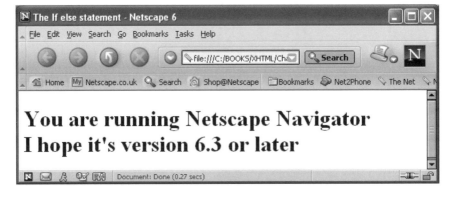

Figure 12.2 Using if else statements.

You can have as many *else if* clauses as you wish and these may contain either a single or compound statement.

The comparison operators

In the examples we have looked at so far, we have only used one comparison operator to test for equality, but JavaScript has the usual set of comparison operators as shown in Table 12.1

Table 12.1 The comparison operators.

Operator	Meaning
==	Is equal to.
>	Is greater than.
<	Is less than.
>=	Is greater than or equal to.
<=	Is less than or equal to.

The long statement below shows how these operators can be used to display a different message depending on the value that the numeric variable *cpuSpeed* is assigned.

```
if (cpuSpeed < 700)
        document.write("Your processor is very slow")
else if (cpuSpeed <= 1000)
```

```
            document.write("Your processor is OK");
    else if (cpuSpeed < 2000)
            document.write("You have a fast processor");
    else if (cpuSpeed >= 2000)
            document.write("Fast computer!!")
```

The result of comparing two quantities is a boolean, that is a true or false value. If a true value is produced the statement following is executed.

The >, >= , < and <= operators should be used with caution when comparing strings, since a comparison is based on the Unicode encoding of strings which is not alphabetical: all of the upper case letters come before all of the lower case letters, so if you compare the strings ("zackery" > "aladdin"), the result is true, that is "zackery is greater than "aladdin". However, if you compare "Zackery" and "aladdin", the result is false, "aladdin" is greater than "Zackery".

The logical operators

If is often necessary to check if more than one condition is met before executing some lines of JavaScript, this can be done by using the logical operators.
There are three logical operators:

- The AND operator &&.
- The OR operator ||.
- The NOT operator !.

We are going to look at these next and see how they are used with the *if else* statement.

The && operator

The logical AND operator && is used to test if two conditions are true, if they are, the statement following is executed, for example:

```
if ((cpuSpeed < 500) && (memory <256))
       document.write("Maybe you should get a new PC");
```

If both of the conditions are met, the following statement is executed and the message is displayed.

The || operator

The logical OR operator || tests to see if either or both of the test conditions are true. If so, the following statement is executed, for example:

```
if ((cpuSpeed < 500) || (memory <256))
       document.write("Maybe you should upgrade");
```

The ! operator

The logical NOT operator ! is applied to a single operand, it converts a boolean operator to its converse, for example:

```
var on = false;
document.write("on is "+ on + " !on is " + !on);
```

displays the message:

```
on is false !on is true
```

The switch construct

When your application has to make a decision you can list as many *if else* clauses as you wish, but this can become confusing. An alternative is to use the *switch* construct. This has two parts:

```
switch (expression) {
       case statements
}
```

The *case* statements have the format:

```
case expression :
        statements
        break;
case expression :
        statements
        break;
case default :
        statements
break;
```

You may have as many case statements as you wish. The *default* statement is optional.

The *switch* expression is calculated and then the first *case* statement is checked to see if it matches this value, if it does, the following statements are executed. The *break* statement makes the application jump to the end of the *switch* construct. If the expression does not match the *case* statement value, the next *case* statement is checked and so on. If none match, the *default* statement (if there is one) is executed.

Note that *case* statement is followed by a *break* statement, if this statement is omitted, the application falls into the lines of code in the next *case* statements until the end of the *switch* construct ends or a *break* statement is met.

An example of using this statement is shown below:

```
<script type = "text/javascript">
<!--
var browserType;
browserType = navigator.appName      //returns the name of your browser
switch(browserType) {
case  "Microsoft Internet Explorer" :
        document.write("Your are running Internet Explorer");
        document.write ("<br />");
        document.write("I hope it's version 6.2 or later");
        break;
case  "Netscape":
        document.write("You are running Netscape Navigator");
        document.write ("<br />");
```

```
                document.write("I hope it's version 6.3 or later");
                break;
default:
                document.write("You are not running Netscape or Explorer");
                document.write ("<br />");
                document.write("I wonder why not?");
                break;
}       //end switch
// -->
</script>
```

This is functionally exactly the same as the version we saw earlier which uses *if else* statements.

This statement is very similar to the *switch* constructs used in Java, however there are some important differences. The type of expression may be either string, boolean, integer, or floating point. It may not be an object or an array.

The *case* statement may be either constants or expressions which are calculated.

Since JavaScript is not as strongly typed as Java the *case* statements do not need to be the same type as the expression in the *switch* statement, however it is advisable that they are.

Looping

We have seen how you can make decisions in JavaScript by using constructs such as *if* statements. Sometimes you may wish the same section of code to be executed more than once. There are a variety of looping constructs which will be familiar if you have programmed in most common high-level languages:

- *while* loops.
- *do..while* loops.
- *for* loops.

We are going to look at each of these.

while loops

The format of a *while* loop is:

```
while (expression)
    statement
```

or its compound form:

```
while (expression) {
    statement
    statement
    ....
}
```

The expression is evaluated and if the expression is true the following statement (or statement block) is executed. The expression is recalculated and checked again. If it is true the following statement is executed. This continues until the expression is false.

An example of using a *while* is shown below. It calculates the diminishing value of a share portfolio - reducing from a million to half by 5% per week. The integer *fundNow* is assigned the value 1 million. The integer *fundFuture* is assigned the value 500,000. The test in the *while* loop is when the *fundNow* is greater or equal to *fundFuture*. When this condition no longer applies, the fund has more than halved in value and the loop ends.

```
<script type = "text/javascript">
<!--
var fundNow, fundFuture, week;
fundNow=1000000;
fundFuture=fundNow/2;
week=1;
while (fundNow >= fundFuture) {
  fundNow = Math.round(fundNow * 0.95);
  document.write("After " + week + " week");
  if (week > 1) document.write("s");
  document.write(" you will have " + fundNow);
  document.write("<br />");
```

```
    week++;
}
// -->
</script>
```

The *Math.round* method rounds the number in brackets to an integer, since when you are losing that much money the cents do not make a lot of difference.   The running application is shown in Figure 12.3.

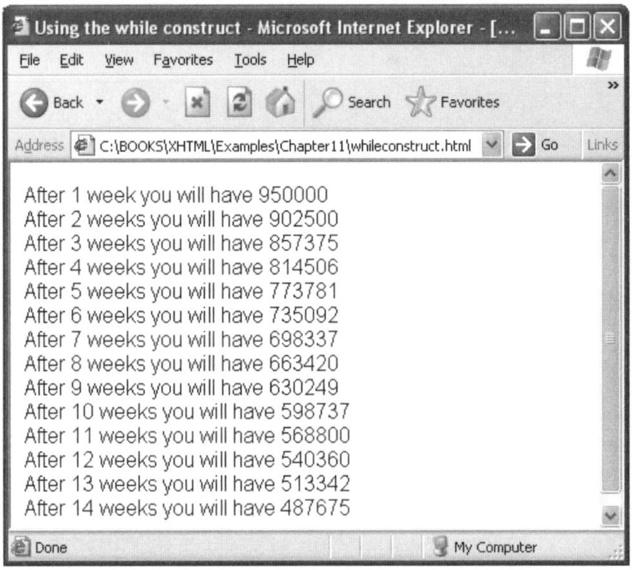

Figure 12.3 Using while loops.

do..while loops

The *do..while* loop is a variant on the *while* loop, the difference is that the test condition is at the end of the loop rather than the start.

The format of the loop is:

```
do
      statement
while (expression);
```

or its compound form:

```
do {
      statement
      statement
      ....
      } while (expression);
```

The previous code has been modified to use a *do* loop rather than a *while* loop and is shown below:

```
<script type = "text/javascript">
<!--
var fundNow, fundFuture, week;
fundNow=1000000;
fundFuture=fundNow/2;
week=1;
do {
      fundNow = Math.round(fundNow * 0.95);
      document.write("After " + week + " week");
      if (week > 1) document.write("s");
      document.write(" you will have " + fundNow);
      week++;
      document.write("<br />");
}
while (fundNow >= fundFuture);
// -->
</script>
```

The output is exactly the same as shown in Figure 12.3

In most cases these two loops can be substituted for each other, but not in every case. Since *do* loops have the test at the end, they are always guaranteed to be executed at least once.

for loops

Since loops often increment a counter, a special loop has been created which has this built in.

The format of the loop is:

```
for (initial statements; test; loop statements)
    statement
```

or its compound form:

```
for (initial statements; text; loop statements) {
    statement
    statement
    ....
}
```

There are three parts to the *for* loop

- initial statements. This is one or more statements, separated by commas, which are only executed the first time the loop is executed.
- test. This test is checked every time the application loops: if it is true, then the loop is executed again; if is false, the loop ends.
- statements. There is one or more statements which are executed every time the loop is executed except for the first time. Usually only one statement is used here.

A variation on our declining share portfolio application is shown below. This uses a *for* loop and produces exactly the same output as the *while* and *do* loops as shown in Figure 12.3.

```
<script type = "text/javascript">
<!--
var fundNow, fundFuture, week;
fundNow=1000000;
fundFuture=fundNow/2;
week=1;
for (week=1; week < 15; week++) {
  fundNow = Math.round(fundNow * 0.95);
```

```
    document.write("After " + week + " week");
    if (week > 1) document.write("s");
    document.write(" you will have " + fundNow);
    document.write("<br />");
}
// -->
</script>
```

The first time the loop is executed, the variable *week* is assigned the value 1, and a check is made to see if this is less than 15. Since it is, the loop is executed. The second time around, the value of week is increased to 2 and the test condition checked again. This is repeated until week is equal to 15, the loop then ends.

There is normally only one initial statement and one loop statement in a *for* loop, but you can have more than one:

```
<script type = "text/javascript">
<!--
var c, d;
for (c=0, d=20; c < d; c+=2, d -= 3)
        document.write("c is " + c + " and d is " + d + "<br />");
// -->
</script>
```

This assigns c the value 0 and d the value 20. Every time the loop is executed, c is increased by 2 and d decreased by 3. The running application is shown in Figure 12.4.

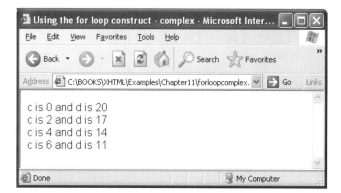

Figure 12.4 Using for loops.

for..in and with statements

We have seen how the reserved word for is used in a loop, but it also has another function for referencing all elements in an array or the properties in an object.

The *with* statement is also a way of implicitly adding an object name to a list of following statements, perhaps to initialize a list of object properties.

Both of these statements are covered in the next chapter which looks at arrays and some of the core JavaScript objects.

Labels

You can label any statement, although there are few occasions when you will need to do so. The syntax is:

```
identifier : statement
```

The identifier can be any legal identifier, it can even be the same as the name of an existing variable or function name, this will not cause a conflict.

The only current use of labels is with *break* and *continue* statements which we are going to look at next.

The break statement

We have already seen the *break* statement in the *switch* construct - to jump to the end of the *switch* statement. The *break* statement can also be used to jump out of loops, for example the script below displays the numbers 0 to 3, since when *c==3* the *break* statement is executed:

```
<script type = "text/javascript">
<!--
var c;
//displays 0 to 3
```

```
for (c=0; c < 6; c++) {
       document.write("c is " + c + "<br />");
       if (c==3) break;
}
// -->
</script>
```

You can also use it to break out of infinite loops which would otherwise not end, for example:

```
<script type = "text/javascript">
<!--
var c;
//displays 0 to 3
c = 0;
while (true) {
       document.write("c is " + c + "<br />");
       if (c==3) break;
       c++;
}
// -->
</script>
```

This also displays the numbers from 0 to 3.

If the loop in which the *break* occurs is a nested loop, that is a loop within another loop, the *break* statement only exits the loop in which it occurs, for example, the script below displays the output shown in Figure 12.5:

```
<script type = "text/javascript">
<!--
var c;
for (c=0; c < 3; c++) {
       for (d=0; d < 3; d++) {
              document.write("c is " + c + " and d is " + d + "<br />");
       }
}
// -->
</script>
```

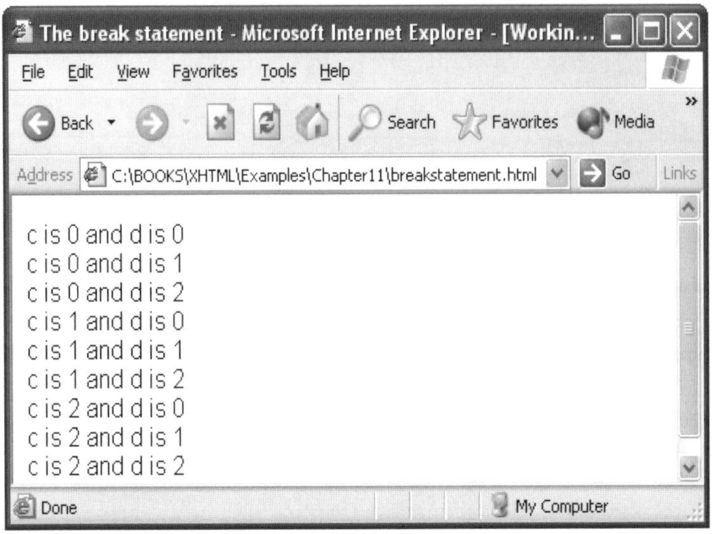

Figure 12.5 Nested for loops.

However, if you add a test condition and *break* statement as shown below:

```
<script type = "text/javascript">
<!--
var c, d;
for (c=0; c < 3; c++) {
     for (d=0; d < 3; d++) {
          if (c == d) break;            // this is the new line
          document.write("c is " + c + " and d is " + d + "<br />");
     }
}
// -->
</script>
```

When *c==d* the inner loop is exited and the output shown in Figure 12.6 is produced. The outer loop is not exited, however it is possible to do this.

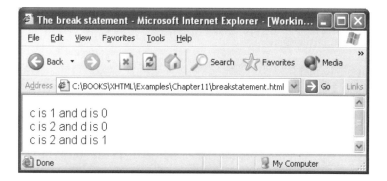

Figure 12.6 Using break statement in a nested loops.

There are two ways to exit from the outer loop as well: you can use another *break* statement in that loop, or alternatively a *break* statement with a label:

```
<script type = "text/javascript">
<!--
var c, d;
exitOuterLoop :
for (c = 0; c < 3; c++) {
      for (d = 0; d < 3; d++) {
            if (c == d) break exitOuterLoop;
      document.write("c is " + c + " and d is " + d + "<br />");
      }
}
// -->
</script>
```

In this script, when *c==d* the outer loop is quit. Since this is the first time the line with the *break* statement is executed *c=0=d*, nothing is displayed.

It is not advisable to routinely exit from loops using *break* statements, it implies that your loop test conditions are not well thought out, however there is one situation in which it is a valid option. If you have encountered some error condition within a deeply nested line of script, which means that it cannot continue in a meaningful way, a *break* statement with a label is a quick and clean way of exiting the loops before taking some action to correct or report the error.

The continue statement

The *continue* statement is very similar to *break* statement, however instead of exiting the current loop entirely, it does not execute the remainder of the loop, but goes on to the next iteration, for example:

```
<script type = "text/javascript">
<!--
var c, d;
for (c = 0; c < 3; c++) {
      for (d = 0; d < 3; d++) {
            if (c == d) continue;
            document.write("c is " + c + " and d is " + d + "<br />");
      }
}
// -->
</script>
```

This produces the output shown in Figure 12.7.

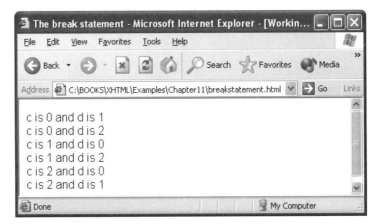

Figure 12.7 The continue statement.

The *continue* statement can also be used with a label.

Chapter

13

JavaScript Core Objects

Introduction

We have looked at the structure of JavaScript and you can already do a great deal using JavaScript which could not be achieved by using XHTML alone, but there are some important aspects of JavaScript which we have not looked at yet. A set of core objects are defined for Java that add a lot of extra functionality, if for example you wish to find out more about the platform that is being used or if you wish to carry out a range of operations, such as sorting lists, manipulating strings or carrying out a wide variety of mathematical operations.

JavaScript also has a set of event handlers which allow you to respond to events such as clicking on a button, or moving the mouse. The response will be much faster than the handling of XHTML forms which we have already seen, since the event is handled locally without reference to the server.

The navigator object

We have already seen the *navigator* object used to identify the browser being used, using its *appName* property. It has a lot of other properties apart from this, some of which are shown in Table 13.1.

Table 13.1 Properties of the navigator object.

Property	Description
appCodeName	The code name of the browser.
appName	The official name of the browser.
appVersion	The version number of the browser
language	The browser language.
platform	A string giving details of the platform on which the browser is being run.
plugins	An array of plug-ins installed on the browser.
userAgent	A string which gives the user-agent header.

These properties give us more information about the

browser and the platform on which it is being run. All the methods return strings or an array of strings.

The JavaScript below can be used to produce the output shown in Figure 13.1, for Internet Explorer v6.0 running under Windows XP Professional operating system.

```
<script type = "text/javascript">
<!--
document.write("navigator.appCodeName : " + navigator.appCodeName + "<br />");
document.write("navigator.appName : " + navigator.appName + "<br />");
document.write("navigator.appVersion : " + navigator.appVersion + "<br />");
document.write("navigator.language : " + navigator.language + "<br />");
document.write("navigator.platform : " + navigator.platform + "<br />");
document.write("navigator.userAgent : " + navigator.userAgent);
// -->
</script>
```

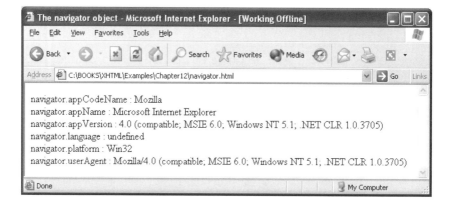

Figure 13.1 The navigator object.

In addition to properties, objects have a set of methods, which are operations which the object can carry out, for example, if we had a string object, we could have a search method which would search for the position of some text within the string object.

The navigator object has a set of methods, which only have patchy support with browsers. The only property which seems to have extensive support is *javaEnabled()*, which returns true if the browser supports Java and false if it does not. For example:

```
<script type = "text/javascript">
<!--
if (navigator.javaEnabled()) document.write("Java is enabled");
 else document.write("Java is not enabled");
// -->
</script>
```

Important JavaScript objects

In addition to the navigator object, some of the most widely used core JavaScript objects are:

- *Date.* Dates occur frequently when dealing with user input. A comprehensive set of methods are provided.
- *Array.* Arrays are a common way of connecting items of the same type.
- *String.* A wide range of methods are provided for all aspects of string manipulation.
- *Math.* Methods provide all of the common mathematical operations you are likely to use.

We are going to look at some of the methods and properties of these objects.

The Date object

You can create *Date* objects in a variety of ways, for example:

```
theDate = new Date ( );
theDate = new Date(milliseconds);
theDate = new Date(dateString);
theDate = new Date(year, month, day, hours, minutes, milliseconds);
```

- The year must be specified in four digit format, for example 2003.

Table 13.2 Methods of *Date* object.

Method	Description
getDate( )	Returns the day of the month of the Date object.
getDay	Returns the day of the week.
getFullYear()	Returns the year in four digits.
getHours( )	Returns the hour.
getMilliseconds( )	Returns the miliseconds.
getMinutes( )	Returns the minutes.
getMonth( )	Returns the month.
getSeconds( )	Returns the seconds.
getTime( )	Returns the internal representation of the Date object in milliseconds.
getTimeZoneOffset( )	Returns the time difference in minutes between the time and the GMT time.
getUTCDate( )	Returns the day of the month in universal time.
getUTCDay( )	Returns the day of the week in universal time.
getUTCFullYear( )	Returns the year in four digits, in universal time.
getUTCHours( )	Returns the hour in universal time.
getUTCMilliseconds( )	Returns the milliseconds in universal time.
getUTCMinutes( )	Returns the minutes in universal time.
getUTCMonth( )	Returns the month in universal time.
getUTCSeconds( )	Returns the seconds in universal time.
setDate(dayOfMonth)	Sets the day of the month.
setFullYear(year)	Sets the year.
setHours(hour)	Sets the hour.
setMilliseconds(ms)	Sets the milliseconds.
setMinutes(min)	Sets the minutes.
setMonth(month)	Sets the month.
setSeconds(sec)	Sets the seconds.
setTime(ms)	Sets the time in milliseconds using the internal representation of the Date object.
setUTCDate(dayOfMonth)	Sets the day of the month in universal time.
setUTCFullYear(year)	Sets the year field in universal time.
setUTCHours(hour)	Sets the hours field in universal time.
setUTCMilliseonds(ms)	Sets the milliseconds in universal time.
setUTCMinutes(min)	Sets the minutes in universal time.
setUTCMonth(month)	Sets the month in universal time.
setUTCSeconds(sec)	Sets the seconds in universal time.
toGMTString( )	Returns a string representing the date in GMT.
toLocaleString( )	Returns a string representing the date in the local time.
toString( )	Returns a string representation of the date.
toUTCString( )	Returns a string representation of the UTC date.
valueOf( )	Converts the date to milliseconds using the internal representation.

- The month is an integer, surprisingly 0 (not 1) is January and eleven is December.
- The day is an integer from 1 to the number of days in the month. This is optional.
- The hour is an integer between 0 and 23. Optional.
- The minutes and seconds are integers between 0 and 59. Both optional.
- The milliseconds are integers between 0 and 999. Optional.

For example:

```
var theDate = new Date(2003,6,15);
```

To get today's date, use the constructor method without attributes:

```
var theDateToday = new Date( );
```

There are a comprehensive set of methods for getting and setting the date, shown in Table 13.2. You could guess what most of these methods do by looking at their name, the only surprise is the format in which dates may be printed out as shown in Figure 13.2.

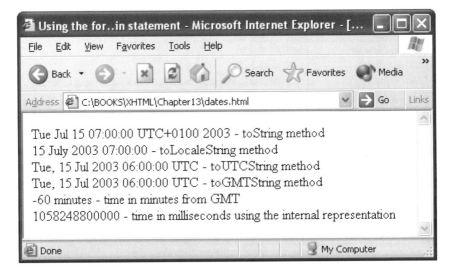

Figure 13.2 Using Date methods.

The JavaScript used to produce this page is shown below:

```
<script type = "text/javascript">
<!--
var theDate = new Date(2003,6,15,7);
document.write(theDate.toString( ) + " - toString method" + "<br />");
document.write(theDate.toLocaleString( ) + " - toLocaleString method" + "<br />");
document.write(theDate.toUTCString( ) + " - toUTCString method" + "<br />");
document.write(theDate.toGMTString( ) + " - toGMTString method" + "<br />");
document.write(theDate.getTimezoneOffset( ) + " minutes - time in minutes from
GMT" + "<br />");
document.write(theDate.getTime( ) + " - time in milliseconds using the internal
representation" + "<br />");
// -->
</script>
```

The Array object

An array is a data structure which is a list of items of the same type, for example a set of marks for a class could be stored in an array of integers.

You can create an *Array* object in a variety of ways: to create an Array object with a length of zero

```
myArray = new Array( )
```

To create an array with a length of 10. The first element is *myArray[0]* the last *myArray[9]*.

```
myArray = new Array(10);
```

You can specify some initial values if you wish:

```
myArray = new Array(2, 3, 4 )
```

This creates an array with three elements set to the given values.

The *length* property gives the number of items in the array, if *length* is 5, the first element is 0 and the last 4. The JavaScript shown below displays the numbers 0 to 4.

```
<script type = "text/javascript">
<!--
var myList = new Array(5);
for (c=0; c<myList.length; c++)
document.write(c +"<br />");
// -->
</script>
```

Arrays can have more than one dimension, for example a timetable could be represented as a two dimensional array:

```
timetable = new Array(20, 30);
```

A set of the methods of *String* objects is given in Table 13.3.

Table 13.3 Methods of *Array* object.

Method	Description
concat(value,..)	Creates and returns an array after adding specified values to an existing array. The original array is unchanged.
join( ) *join(separator)*	Converts each element into a string and then concatenates them. If a separator is not specified a comma is used. The original array is unchanged.
pop( )	Deletes the last element of an array and returns the resulting array.
push(value,...)	Adds elements to an array and returns the resulting array.
reverse( )	Reverses the order of elements in an array.
shift( )	Removes the first element of an array and returns it.
slice(start, end)	Returns the portion of an array between a start and finish index. A negative index specifies a position from the end of the array. The original array is unchanged.
sort( ) *sort(orderfunction)*	Returns the array sorted by numerical or alphabetical order.
splice(start, deleteCount, value..)	Deletes zero or more elements, starting at the specified starting position and replaces them by a list of values.
toString( )	Converts the array to a string.
unshift(value,..)	Inserts a set of values at the start of the array.

We are going to see most of these methods in action in the next example. Note that some of the lines of script are too long to fit onto the page, but if you try them for yourself they must be typed as a single line to work.

- We start first by declaring and displaying the original array:

```
<script type = "text/javascript">
<!--
var a = new Array("a","b","c","d","e");
document.write(a.toString( )+ " - toString method - The original array " +"<br />");
```

This displays a, b, c, d, e.

- The literals f and g are added to the string using the *concat* method:

```
document.write(a.concat("f", "g")+ " - concat method - add f and g - original array
unchanged "+ "<br />");
```

This displays a, b, c, d, e, f, g. The original array is unchanged.

- The *join* method is used to separate the array items with the + character:

```
document.write(a.join("+")+ " - join method - returns a string with + as the separator -
original array unchanged "+ "<br />");
```

This displays a + b + c + d + e. The original array is unchanged.

- The last item in the array is removed from the original array:

```
a.pop( );
document.write(a.toString( )+ " - the array after using the pop method to remove e"
+"<br />");
```

This displays a, b, c, d.

- The literal f is added to the array:

```
a.push("f");
document.write(a.toString( )+" - the array after using the push method to add f"
+"<br />");
```

This displays a, b, c, d, f.

- The order of items in the array is reversed:

```
document.write(a.reverse( )+ " - reverse method - original array updated"+ "<br />");
```

This displays f, d, c, b, a.

- The *shift* method returns the first element in the array and removes it from the array.

```
document.write(a.shift( )+ " - shift method - return the first element - original array
updated"+ "<br />");
```

f is displayed.

- The original array is displayed to show the removal of f.

```
document.write(a.toString( )+ " - the array after using the shift method to remove f"
+"<br />");
```

This displays d, c, b, a.

- The *slice* method returns a section of the array:

```
document.write(a.slice(2,3)+ " - slice method - returns a section of the array - original
array unchanged" + "<br />");
```

This displays b.

- The original array is shown unchanged:

```
document.write(a.toString( )+ " - the array after using the slice method" +"<br />");
```

This displays d, c, b, a.

- The *sort* method is used to show the array elements in alphabetical order:

```
document.write(a.sort()+ " - sort method - sorts the array - original array updated"+
"<br />");
```

This displays a, b, c, d.

- The *splice* method is used to delete elements 1 and 2 (that is a and b) and replace them with the literal z:

```
a.splice(1,2,"z");
document.write(a.toString()+ " - the array after using the splice method to delete 2
elements and replacing with z"+ "<br />");
```

This displays a, z, d.

- Finally the *unshift* is used to add the literal x to the start of the array which is displayed.

```
a.unshift("x");
document.write(a.toString()+ " - the array after using the unshift method to add x at
the start "+ "<br />");
// -->
</script>
```

This displays x, a, z, d.

The complete listing is shown below:

```
<script type = "text/javascript">
<!--
var a = new Array("a","b","c","d","e");
document.write(a.toString( )+ " - toString method - The original array "+ "<br />");
document.write(a.concat("f", "g")+ " - concat method - add f and g - original array
unchanged "+ "<br />");
document.write(a.join("+")+ " - join method - returns a string with + as the separator -
original array unchanged "+ "<br />");
a.pop( );
document.write(a.toString( )+ " - the array after using the pop method to remove e"+
"<br />");
a.push("f");
document.write(a.toString( )+" - the array after using the push method to add f"+
"<br />");
document.write(a.reverse( )+ " - reverse method - original array updated"+ "<br />");
document.write(a.shift( )+ " - shift method - return the first element - original array
updated"+ "<br />");
document.write(a.toString( )+ " - the array after using the shift method to remove f"+
"<br />");
document.write(a.slice(2,3)+ " - slice method - returns a section of the array - original
array unchanged" + "<br />");
document.write(a.toString( )+ " - the array after using the slice method" + "<br />");
document.write(a.sort()+ " - sort method - sorts the array - original array updated"+
"<br />");
a.splice(1,2,"z");
document.write(a.toString()+ " - the array after using the splice method to delete 2
elements and replacing with z"+ "<br />");
a.unshift("x");
document.write(a.toString()+ " - the array after using the unshift method to add x at
the start "+ "<br />");
// -->
</script>
```

This script produces the page shown in Figure 13.3.

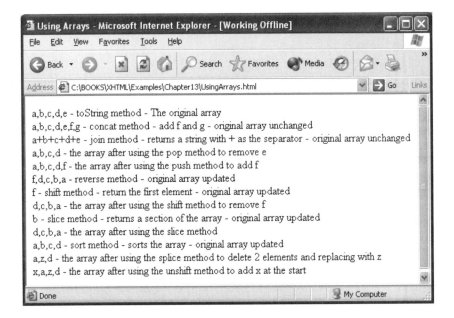

Figure 13.3 Using Array methods.

The for..in construct

A useful way of referencing all of the elements in an array is to use the *for..in* construct - which should not be confused with the *for* loop construct. The syntax of this construct is:

```
for (variable in objectOrArray)
    statement
```

- The *variable* may be the element of an array or an object property.
- The *objectOrArray* may be either an object or an array name.

In the example below an array, called *myArray* used. The name of the variable is *c*.

```
<script type = "text/javascript">
<!--
```

```
var c;
var myArray = new Array("a","b","c","d","e");
for (c in myArray) {
document.write(myArray[c] + "<br />");
}
// -->
</script>
```

This prints the letters *a* to *e*, one below the other.

If you wish you can use the name of an object, although there are some limitations, for example:

```
for (p in navigator) {
    document.write(navigator[p] + "<br />");
    }
```

This will display the properties of the *navigator* object, however, the order is unpredictable. In addition, some properties are non-enumerable, and are not displayed, so this construct should be used with caution for objects.

The with construct

A useful construct which can save some typing and therefore help to reduce errors is the *with* construct. This has the general form:

```
with (object)
    statement
```

The name of the object is implicitly placed in front of the following statements, for example:

```
<script type = "text/javascript">
<!--
var theTime = new Date();
document.write(theTime.toLocaleString() + "<br />");
with (theTime) {
    setHours(0);
    setMinutes(0);
    setSeconds(0);
    setMilliseconds(0);
```

```
    }
document.write(theTime.toLocaleString() + "<br />");
// -->
</script>
```

The methods, *setHours*, *setMinutes* and so on refer to the *theTime* object stated in the *with* statement. The output produced by this script is shown in Figure 13.4.

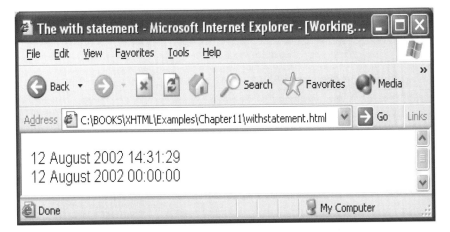

Figure 13.4 The with construct.

The String object

The *String* object has an extensive set of properties for formatting and manipulating strings.

You can create a *String* object in a variety of ways, for example:

```
var mystring = "Hello Bobby";
```

or

```
var mystring = new String( );
```

A set of the methods of *String* objects is given in Table 13.4.

Table 13.4 Methods of *String* object.

Method	Description
anchor(name)	Returns the string enclosed within an XHTML *a* element.
big( )	Returns the string enclosed in a *big* element.
blink( )	Returns the string enclosed in a *blink* element.
bold( )	Returns the string enclosed in a *b* element.
charAt(n)	Returns the character at the specified position.
charCodeAt(n)	Returns the Unicode encoding of the character at the specified position.
concat(value,..)	Concatenates two strings to return a single string.
fixed( )	Returns a copy of the string in a *tt* element (that is with a fixed pitch font).
fontcolor(colour)	Returns a copy of the string with a *font* element specifying the colour.
fontsize(size)	Returns a copy of the string with a *font* element specifying the font size as a value between 1 and 7.
indexOf(substr) *indexOf(substr,start)*	Returns the position of the first occurrence of a string within the *String* object.
italics( )	Returns the string enclosed in an *i* element.
lastIndexOf(substr) *lastIndexOf(substr,start)*	Returns the position of the last occurrence of a string, passed to the method ,within the *String* object.
link(href)	Returns an *a* element with the *href* attribute set to the URL passed to the method.
match(regexp)	Carries out pattern matching based on a regular expression passed to the method.
replace(regexp,replace)	Carries out a search and replace operation.
search(regexp)	Returns the position of a string passed to the method in the String object.
slice(start,end)	Returns the string between the two index positions.
small( )	Returns the string enclosed in a *small* element.
split(delimiter)	Returns an array of strings split on the basis of a delimiting string passed to the method.
strike( )	Returns the string enclosed in a *strike* element.
sub( )	Returns the string enclosed in a *sub* element.
substr(start,length)	Returns a string between a start index and a specified numbers of characters. If the start index is negative it is the position from the end of the string.
substring(start, finish)	Returns a string between a start index and finish index. The start index may not be negative.
sup( )	Returns the string enclosed in a *sup* element.
toLowerCase( )	Returns a copy of the string in lowercase.
toUpperCase( )	Returns a copy of the string in uppercase.

An example of some of these methods in use is shown below:

```
<script type = "text/javascript">
<!--
var mystring = "Hello Bobby";
document.write(mystring + "<br />");
document.write(mystring.big( ) + "<br />");
document.write(mystring.small( ) + "<br />");
document.write(mystring.italics( ) + "<br />");
document.write(mystring.toUpperCase( ) + "<br />");
document.write(mystring.toLowerCase( ) + "<br />");
document.write(mystring.fontsize(7) + "<br />");
document.write(mystring.fontcolor("red") + "<br />");
// -->
</script>
```

This JavaScript produces the document shown in Figure 13.5.

Figure 13.5 String methods.

A useful property is *length*, for example:

```
var mystring = "Hello Bobby";
document.write(mystring.length);
```

The length of this string is 11 characters.

The set of string manipulation methods is extensive, for example:

```
s = "a,b,c,d,e";
document.write("First occurrence of the , character is at " + s.indexOf(",")+ "<br />");
document.write("Last occurrence of the , character is at "+s.lastIndexOf(",")+"<br />");
a = new Array( );
a = s.split(",");
for (c = 0; c<a.length; c++)
        document.write(a[c]);
```

This produces the output shown in Figure 13.6.

First occurrence of the , character is at 1
Last occurrence of the , character is at 7
abcde

Figure 13.6 *Manipulating strings.*

The Math object

There are a range of useful mathematical constants and methods, shown in Tables 13.5 and 13.6. We have already seen how to carry out basic operations such as addition and multiplication, but these methods give you far greater capabilities.

Table 13.5 Constants of the *Math* object.

Constant	Description
Math.E	The constant e.
Math.LN10	The natural logarithm of 10.
Math.LN2	The natural logarithm of 2.
Math.LOG10E	The base 10 log of e.
Math.LOG2E	The base 2 logarithm of 2.
Math.PI	The constant pi.
Math.SQRT1_2	1 divided by the square of 2.
Math.SQRT2	The square root of 2.

An example of using the constant for pi:

```
document.write("The area of a circle or radius 3 is " + Math.PI*3*3);
```

The output is shown in Figure 13.7.

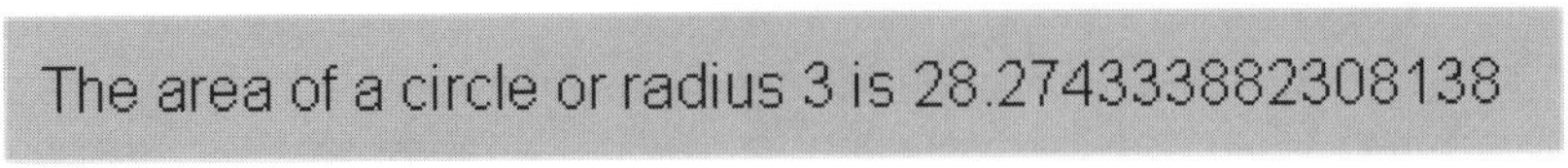

The area of a circle or radius 3 is 28.274333882308138

Figure 13.7 *Using the Math constants.*

There are also a set of *Math* methods which cover all of the most popular mathematical operations. These are shown in Table 13.6.

Table 13.6 Methods of the *Math* object.

Method	Description
Math.abs(x)	Returns the absolute value.
Math.acos(x)	Returns the arccosine value.
Math.asin(x)	Returns the arcsine value.
Math.atan(x)	Returns the arctangent value.
Math.atan2(y,x)	Returns the arctangent between a point(x,y) and the X axis.
Math.ceil(x)	Returns the closest integer to the value specified.
Math.cos(x)	Returns the cosine of an angle.
Math.exp(x)	Returns the e^x value.
Math.floor(x)	Returns the value rounded down to the nearest integer.
Math.log(x)	Returns the natural log.
Math.max(a, b)	Returns the larger of two given values.
Math.min(a, b)	Returns the smaller of two given values.
Math.pow(x, y)	Returns the value of x^y.
Math.random( )	Returns a random number between 0.0 and 1.0.
Math.round(x)	Returns the integer closest to the given value.
Math.sin(x)	Returns the sine of the given value.
Math.sqrt(x)	Returns the square root of the given value.
Math.tan(x)	Returns the tangent of the given value.

These methods are not the same as the other methods we have seen. In object-oriented terms they are static methods, and rather than preceding the method name by the name of an object we have created, the method name is always preceded by the name of the *Math* class. For example we could improve our previous example which calculates the area of a circle of radius 3 by using the *Math.pow()* method, to give exactly the same output:

```
document.write("The area of a circle or radius 3 is " + Math.PI*Math.pow(3,2) +"<br />");
```

Chapter 14

Handling Events

Introduction

If you want to make your web pages really interesting, you can increase the interactivity between the pages and the user by responding to the users' actions. An important aspect of JavaScript is that you can write handlers which will respond to events which happen on your web pages, such as displaying a help message when the mouse moves over a link, or validating the input from a form.

JavaScript can respond to a comprehensive set of events. In this chapter we are going to look at these and see how you can write JavaScript to respond to them.

The mouse events

The first event handlers we are going to look at are the mouse events, these are listed in Table 14.1. This table also lists the objects which support these events.

Table 14.1 JavaScript mouse events.

Event handler	Description	Objects
onclick	Occurs when the mouse is clicked on a supporting object.	document, button, checkbox, radio, link, reset, submit.
ondblclick	Occurs when the mouse is double clicked on a supporting object.	document, link, area.
onmousedown	Occurs when a mouse button is clicked over a supporting object.	button, document, link.
onmouseout	Occurs when the mouse is moved off a supporting object.	area, layer, link.
onmouseover	Occurs when the mouse is moved onto a supporting object.	area, layer, link.
onmouseup	Occurs when a mouse button is released.	button, document, link.

The event which is produced by an action depends on that action and also on where it occurs, for example, the click event occurs when you click on a link, but clicking on a text area element does not produce any event.

To see how the event handlers work we are going to look at the *onclick* event. This event occurs when an object which supports this event, such as a link, is clicked. In this example, when the click event occurs, the *onclick* event handler runs. In this case it uses the *alert* function to display an alert box.

```
<a href="Chocolatenews.html" onclick = "alert('you have clicked the link');
return true;">
Chocolate News<br /><br />
</a>
```

Note the use of single quotes to delimit the text displayed by the alert box. These are used since the whole statement itself is already within double quotes.

When the link is clicked the alert box shown in Figure 14.1 is displayed.

Figure 14.1 The onclick event.

A return type of true has been added to indicate the successful status of the event handling. In this case it is not useful. However, when dealing with an event such as the *onsubmit* event handler a return of false could indicate that the form had failed the validation and should not be submitted to the server for processing. If the event handler is displaying some information in the status bar, a return of true prevents the text being overwritten by the browser.

If you wish, you can handle more than one event for an object and also execute a function in response to the event, for example:

```
<script type = "text/javascript">
<!--
function handler(event) {
      window.status = "The " + event + " has occurred";
}
// -->
</script>
<p>
<a href="www.breakawayflyingschool.com"
onmouseover ="handler('onmouseover'); return true;"
onmouseup ="handler('onmouseup'); return true"
onmousedown ="handler('onmousedown'); return true"
onmouseout ="handler('onmouseout'); return true">
<img src="transparent.gif" alt ="aeroplane" />
</a>
</p>
```

The function called handler is passed some text which is
the name of the event which has occurred. A message is
displayed in the status window indicating the name of the
event. In the XHTML the function is called in response to
every event - and passed some text which indicates what
event has happened.

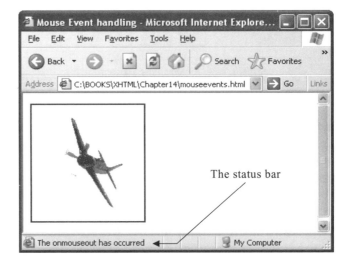

Figure 14.2 The onclick event.

This is shown in Figure 14.2 just after the *onmouseout* event has occurred.

Linking events to controls such as buttons is done in the same way, for example, to respond to the *onclick* event for a button:

```
<p>
<input type = "button" name = "btnexit" value = " Exit "
onclick = "alert('Are you sure?');
return true;" />
</p>
```

This produces the display shown in Figure 14.3 when the button is clicked.

Figure 14.3 The onclick event for a button control.

The keyboard events

There are three keyboard events which are shown in Table 14.2. In addition the *onselect* event has been included.

We can use the keyboard event handlers in a similar way to the mouse events, for example with the text control.

Table 14.2 JavaScript keyboard events.

Event handler	Description	Objects
onkeydown	Occurs when any key is pressed.	document, image, link, text, textarea.
onkeypress	Occurs when any key is pressed.	document, image, link, text, textarea.
onkeyup	Occurs when any key is released.	document, image, link, text, textarea.
onselect	Occurs when text is selected within a text or textarea control.	text, textarea.

```
<script type = "text/javascript">
<!--
function handler(event) {
      window.status = "The " + event + " has occurred";
}
// -->
</script>
<p>
<input type = "text" name = "firstname" size="25"
onkeyup = "handler('onkeyup'); return true"
onkeydown = "handler('onkeydown'); return true"
onkeypress = "handler('onpress'); return true" />
First name<br />
</p>
```

The function called *handler* which we looked at in the previous example is used again to display the last event in the status bar. The page produced by this XHTML is shown in Figure 14.4.

Figure 14.4 *The keyboard events for a text control.*

The document and window events

The document events apply to the loading, unloading and resizing of the document window. They are shown in Table 14.3.

Table 14.3 JavaScript document events.

Event handler	Description	Objects
onload	Occurs when a window has finished loading.	window.
onunload	Occurs when a window has finished unloading.	window.
onresize	Occurs when a window or frame is resized.	window, frame.

The following example shows how these handlers can be used to detect the *onload* event.

```
<body onload ="handler('onload'); return true;"
      onunload ="handler('onunload'); return true" >
<script type = "text/javascript">
<!--
function handler(event) {
      window.status ="The " + event + " has occurred";
}
// -->
</script>
</body>
```

The form events

There are two events which are related to forms, they are shown in Table 14.4.

If the return value from the *onreset* or *onsubmit* event handlers is false that action is cancelled. This is particularly for checking that the user has completed all of the fields in a form correctly before it is submitted to the server or processing. We are going to look at how to carry out validation on a form before it is submitted.

Table 14.4 JavaScript document events.

Event handler	Description	Objects
onreset	Occurs when a form is reset.	form.
onsubmit	Occurs when form data is submitted to the server.	form.

Verifying form data

When the *submit* button is clicked, the data given in a form is sent to the server for validation. If the data is incorrect or incomplete an error message can be returned, however it is best to minimize traffic across the network and more efficient to perform some basic validation locally. In the example shown running in Figure 14.5, the user is prompted for a username and password.

Figure 14.5 Validation text fields.

When the login button is clicked, the two input fields are checked to see if either or both are empty. If they are, the alert box shown in Figure 14.6 is displayed.

Figure 14.6 Failed alert box.

If neither are empty the alert box shown in Figure 14.7 is displayed.

Figure 14.7 Success alert box.

The XHTML which produces the form is shown below:

```
<form method = "post" action = "null" onsubmit = "return handler(this);">
<h1>
Please login
</h1>
<p>
<input type ="text" name ="Username" size="25" /> User name<br />
<input type="password" name="IDCode" maxlength="10" size="10" />Password<br />
</p>
<p>
<input type ="submit" value = "  Login   " />
</p>
</form>
```

This is straightforward apart from the first line:

```
<form method = "post" action = "null"; onsubmit = "return handler(this);">
```

When the *submit* button is clicked, the event handler is called. This is a function called *handler*. The identifier *this* identifies the name of the current form. It is passed to the function. The function returns either true, in which case the submission can proceed, or false, in which case it does not. In the handler function the contents of the text and password control are checked and if either is empty, the error alert box is displayed and false is returned to prevent submission to the server. In this example, the *action* attribute has been assigned to null, since it makes the testing of the validation code easier. When this is working satisfactorily the correct value of the *action* attribute can be inserted.

The handler function is shown below:

```
<script type = "text/javascript">
<!--
function handler(PCForm) {
var empty=0;
for (var c=0; c<PCForm.length; c++) {
    var e = PCForm.elements[c];
    if ((e.type == "text") || (e.type == "password")) {
        if ((e.value == null) || (e.value == "")) empty++;
        }
    }
    if (empty > 0) {
        alert("Unable to submit - You must type your username and password");
        return false;
    }
    alert("Click to proceed");
    return true;
}
// -->
</script>
```

PCForm is the name of the current form in this function. This is a local name which is only valid within this function.

The number of controls is given by the *length* property, that is *PCForm.length*.

The *elements* property is an array which represents the items on the form. The first control is given by

PCForm.elements[0], the last element on the form is given by *PCForm.elements[PCForm.length-1]*.

To save typing, *e* is given the value of *PCForm.elements[c]*. The identifier called *e*. The *type* attribute of each element identifies what sort it is, for example a text control or a password control.

The *value* property of each of these two controls gives the text it contains, if either is empty, the integer *empty* is incremented.

After checking every control on the form, if either or both are empty the error dialog is displayed and false returned. If neither are empty, the submit alert box is displayed and true is returned.

A similar approach can be used when checking other types of data, for example verifying that a text field is numeric.

The application we are going to look at next is shown in Figure 14.8. It has two text fields. A value in dollars is typed into the first control and when the *convert* button is clicked, the value in Euros is displayed. The *Euro* text control is read only. If a non-numeric value is typed into the *Dollar* text control an error dialog is displayed and the *Euro* text control is cleared.

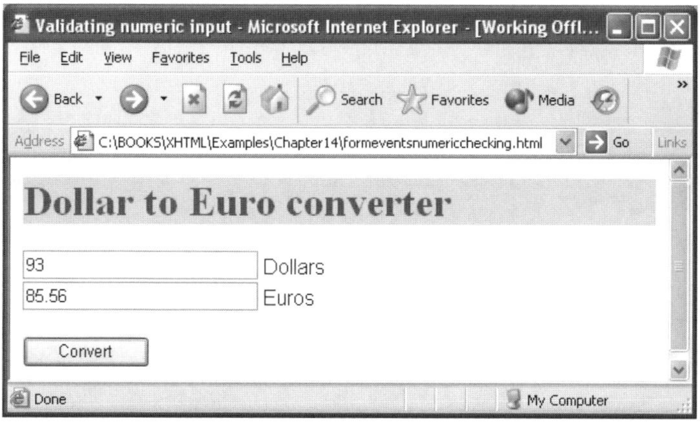

Figure 14.8 Validating numeric fields.

The form is very similar to other forms we have seen. The *readonly* attribute of the lower text control is used to prevent typing into that control. When the *submit* button is clicked, the handler function is called. It is passed *this*, the current form. The XHTML code for the form is shown below:

```
<form method = "post" action = "null" onsubmit = "return handler(this);">
<h1>
Dollar to Euro converter
</h1>
<p>
<input type ="text" name ="dollars" size="25"/> Dollars<br/>
<input type ="text" name ="euros" readonly ="readonly" size="25" /> Euros<br />
</p>
<p>
<input type ="submit" value = "  Convert  " />
</p>
</form>
```

The JavaScript for the handler function is shown below:

```
<script type = "text/javascript">
<!--
function handler(CurrencyForm) {
var error = false;
var euro=0;        //the position of the euro control in elements
var dollarsInEuro=0.92;       // the conversion rate
for (var c=0; c<CurrencyForm.length; c++) {
      var e = CurrencyForm.elements[c];
      if ((e.name == "dollars")) {
            var dollar = parseFloat(e.value);
            if (isNaN(dollar)) error =true;
            }
      if (e.name == "euros") var euro = c;
      }
      if (error) {
            alert("Input a valid number");
            CurrencyForm.elements[euro].value = "";
            return false;
      }
      CurrencyForm.elements[euro].value = dollar * dollarsInEuro;
      return true; // submit to the server
```

```
}
// -->
</script>
```

As before each control of the form is checked by looking at the *CurrencyForm.element* array, from the first element, zero, to the last, *CurrencyForm.length-1*.

The *name* property is checked to see if the current control is the *Dollars* control where the amount is entered. If it is, the *parseFloat* method is used to attempt to convert the string value (*e.value*) into a floating point number. There is one weakness to this method, if non-numeric characters are added to the end of an otherwise valid number, they will simply be ignored and the input string will be accepted as a valid number. This could be dealt with, but it would require further processing.

The *isNaN* method returns true if the conversion to a floating point number has been successful, and *false* if it has not. A failure to convert means than a non-numeric value was typed into the *dollars* text field and the error boolean is assigned to *true*.

The number of the element where the *euro* text control is stored is recorded and assigned to the integer *c*.

After this checking if the error boolean is true a warning alert box is displayed and the euro text field is cleared.

If the error boolean is false, the amount in dollars is multiplied by the conversion factor and the resulting amount is copied into the value property of the euro text field, where it is displayed.

The focus events

There are three events which are related to the focus on an item. They are shown in Table 14.5.

Table 14.5 JavaScript document events.

Event handler	Description	Supported by
onblur	Occurs when a supporting object loses focus.	select, text, textarea.
onchange	Occurs when a supporting object loses focus and has changed since it gained the focus.	select, text, textarea.
onfocus	Occurs when a supporting object gains the focus.	select, text, textarea.

The *onfocus* event occurs when an object gains the focus. Its converse is the *onblur* event which occurs when an object such as a link or a text field loses focus.

The *onchange* event is similar to the *onblur* event, it occurs when an item both loses control and has also changed.

Chapter

15

Deprecated and Valid Elements

Introduction

HTML 4 is backwards compatible with HTML 2, 3.2 and 4.0 and unless elements have been specifically deprecated in XHTML you can still use them safely. Some formatting elements such as *big* although not specifically deprecated are no longer the preferred way of formatting text - style sheets should be used instead. If you are writing documents which will be viewed with recent versions of the browser all formatting should be done with style sheets.

We have met many XHTML elements in this book, but it is useful to have a list of deprecated and valid elements for XHTML 1.1.

Deprecated elements

Table 15.1 shows a list of deprecated elements in XHTML 1.1 which should be avoided. Browsers will recognize them, but your document will fail the W3C validation.

Table 15.1 Deprecated elements in XHTML 1.1.

Element	Description
applet	Reference a Java applet.
basefont	Base font size.
center	Centers an item in the browser.
dir	Directory list.
font	Specifies the font.
isindex	Prompt for input.
menu	Menu list.
s	Strikethrough text.
strike	Strikethrough text.
u	Underline text.

Current XHTML elements

All the current valid elements are listed in Table 15.2. that is the elements which have not been explicitly deprecated.

A few elements which are highly browser specific, such as the *layer* element which can be used in Netscape 4 and later (for specifying a z-order for items within a document) are not included.

Table 15.2 Valid XHTML 1.1 elements.

Element	Description	Empty/not empty
a	The Anchor element. Used to specify a link to another location.	Not empty.
abbr	An abbreviation in a document.	Not empty.
acronym	An acronym in a document.	Not empty.
address	Displays enclosed text in italics, may be used to display contact information.	Not empty.
area	Specifies a region within an image map.	Not empty.
b	Displays text in bold.	Not empty.
base	Gives a URL from which all relative URLs are based.	Empty.
bdo	Specifies the direction text is to be displayed, from left to right or right to left. Used with languages such as Arabic which is written right to left.	Not empty.
big	Displays text in a larger font. A style sheet is the preferred method of doing this.	Not empty.
blink	Makes text blink on and off. A style sheet is the preferred method of doing this.	Not empty.
blockquote	Useful for displaying text which is quoted. Use the q element for quotes in-line in the text.	Not empty.
body	Specifies the body part of the document.	Not empty.
br	Inserts a line break.	Empty.
button	Specifies a submit, resit or image button.	Not empty.
caption	Provides a caption for a table when used within the table element.	Not empty.
cite	Useful for displaying a citation such as a reference.	Not empty.
code	Useful for showing a line of program code in-line in the text. Use the pre element for larger amounts of code.	Not empty.
col	Specifies column properties in a table.	Empty.
colgroup	Specifies the properties of a group of columns.	Not empty.
dd	Definition within a definition list element dl.	Not empty.
del	Useful for marking text for deletion.	Not empty.
dfn	Useful when providing a definition.	Not empty.
div	A break or division within a document.	Not empty.
dl	A definition list which contains dt and dl elements.	Not empty.
dt	An item in a definition list.	Not empty.

em	Emphasizes text by using bolding or italics.	Not empty.
fieldset	Links a group of form controls.	Not empty.
form	Provides a container for input controls.	Not empty.
frame	Specifies a frame within a frameset.	Empty.
frameset	Defines frame attributes.	Not empty.
h1	Header level 1. The largest header.	Not empty.
h2	Header level 2.	Not empty.
h3	Header level 3.	Not empty.
h4	Header level 4.	Not empty.
h5	Header level 5.	Not empty.
h6	Header level 6. The smallest header.	Not empty.
head	Specifies document header information.	Not empty.
hr	Draws a horizontal line.	Empty.
html	This element contains the entire XHTML document.	Not empty.
i	Displays text in italics.	Not empty.
iframe	Creates a floating frame.	Not empty.
img	Displays a specified image.	Empty.
input	Defines an input control within a form.	Empty.
kbd	Allows text to be typed from the keyboard.	Not empty.
label	Displays non-changing text in a form.	Not empty.
legend	Used within a fieldset element to specify descriptive text.	Not empty.
li	A list element.	Not empty.
link	Specifies a link between the current document and another file such as a style sheet.	Empty.
map	Defines a container for a map.	Not empty.
meta	Used to provide information to search engines about the document content.	Empty.
noframes	If a browser does not support frames this element is executed.	Not empty.
noscript	If a browser does not support scripts this element is executed.	Not empty.
object	References an object such as a Java applet or ActiveX object.	Not empty.
ol	Ordered list.	Not empty.
p	A paragraph.	Not empty.
param	Parameters which are passed to an embedded object.	Empty.
pre	Preformatted text such as a more than one line of computer code. Use the code element for showing code in-line in the text.	Not empty.
q	Used for quotes in-line in text. For larger amounts of text use the blockquote element.	Not empty.
samp	Sample of program output.	Not empty.
script	Contains scripting code.	Not empty.

select	A selection list control within a form.	Not empty.
small	Displays text in a small font.	Not empty.
span	Specifies a block of the document to which specified style sheet commands are applied.	Not empty.
strong	Displays text in an emphasized way, usually in bold.	Not empty.
style	Contains style sheet definitions.	Not empty.
sub	Displays text as a subscript.	Not empty.
sup	Displays text as a superscript.	Not empty.
table	Defines a table.	Not empty.
tbody	Defines the body of the table.	Not empty.
td	Defines a table cell.	Not empty.
textarea	A multi-line text input control within a form.	Not empty.
tfoot	Defines the footer section in a table.	Not empty.
th	Defines table headings.	Not empty.
thead	Defines the header section in a table.	Not empty.
title	The document title. This appears in the browser title bar.	Not empty.
tr	Defines a row in a table.	Not empty.
tt	Displays text in a monospaced , 'teletype' font.	Not empty.
ul	Unordered or bulleted list.	Not empty.
var	A variable which is supplied by user input.	Not empty.

Index